Afro-American and East German Fiction

D1825226

American University Studies

Series III
Comparative Literature

Vol. 4

PETER LANG
New York · Berne · Frankfort on the Main

Vernessa C. White

Afro-American
and East German Fiction

A Comparative Study of Alienation, Identity and the Development of Self

PETER LANG
New York · Berne · Frankfort on the Main

Library of Congress Cataloging in Publication Data

White, Vernessa C., 1951–
   Afro-American and East German fiction.

   (American University Studies. Series III, Comparative
literature; v. 4)
   Bibliography: p.
   1. American fiction – Afro-American authors – History
and criticism. 2. German fiction – Germany (East) –
History and criticism. 3. American fiction – 20th century
– History and criticism. 4. German fiction – 20th century
– History and criticism. 5. Literature, Comparative –
American and German. 6. Literature, Comparative – German
and American. 7. Alienation (Social psychology) in
literature. 8. Identity (Psychology) in literature.
9. Self in literature. I. Title. II. Series.

PS153.N5W44 1983   813'.54'09896   83-48138
ISBN 0-8204-0016-5
ISSN 0724-1445

CIP-Kurztitelaufnahme der Deutschen Bibliothek

White, Vernessa C.:
Afro-American and East German fiction: a
comparative study of alienation, identity and
the development of self / Vernessa C. White. –
New York; Berne; Frankfort on the Main:
Lang, 1983.
   (American University Studies: Ser. 3,
   Comparative literature; Vol. 4)
   ISBN 0-8204-0016-5

NE: American University Studies / 03

© Peter Lang Publishing Inc., New York 1983

Printed by Lang Druck Inc., Liebefeld/Berne (Switzerland)

TABLE OF CONTENTS

ACKNOWLEDGMENTS

While it is impossible to name here all those to whom I am indebted for their help in this research project, I wish to thank my family, teachers, and friends, particularly my mother, Lloyd, and Leon for the encouragement given throughout the years. I owe a special vote of thanks to Thomas K. Brown, who believed in me and guided me, and Robert O. Weiss, who taught me the importance of believing in myself. Finally I would like to acknowledge the generosity of the Andrew W. Mellon Foundation, which made it possible for me to complete this dissertation.

FOREWORD

In 1972, with the blessing of my academic advisor, Thomas Brown, I traveled abroad to immerse myself in German culture for a few months. My destination was West Berlin, where, for the duration of my stay in Germany, I lived with the Hildebrandts, the rather Bohemian friends of Tom Brown, and an anything-but-average German family. While all the Hildebrandts figured highly in making my undertaking a success, the influence of Dr. Rainier Hildebrandt, head of the clan, made a particularly lasting impression upon me, and helped to shape my own political and social outlook.

Contemporary art critic, author, and anti-communist political activist, Rainer (along with a few of his professional associates) was the first to introduce me to the topics of East German politics, art, and literature. It was he who convinced me to spend as much time as possible in East Berlin in order to compare it with its Western sister-city, which enjoys the unique situation of being the only capitalist center located entirely within communist borders. I followed Rainer's advice and made the subway trip to East Berlin on a regular basis. My interpretations of life in the East - made from the standpoint of a twenty-year-old, Afro-American female - were duly compared with conditions in West Berlin and the United States, as I understood them. Those early observations stimulated an interest in East-West, Marxist-capitalist relationships that deepened with the passage of time. The interpretations of the initial comparisons, coupled with others I made over the years, have been developed here into my doctoral dissertation.

INTRODUCTION

Preliminary Remarks

One of the most extensively used catchwords of our time, "revolution" is employed throughout the world to flavor the political oratory and rhetoric of countless factions. A word which characterizes this century, its extensive usage has resulted in various meanings or interpretations of the concept. A standard reference like the Encyclopaedia Brittanica, for example, defines revolution as a challenge (be it political or otherwise) to the established order, and the eventual establishment of a new order, radically different from its predecessor. To some, revolution has come to mean a sudden and major alteration in government or related structures, generally violent in nature, and largely spontaneous. For others, revolution signifies, even embodies, liberation itself; it is a spiritual upheaval through which a group or an individual seeks to establish a new foundation for its existence. Thus, those inclined toward the latter definition see the revolutionary process as part of the unfolding of human potentiality rather than a concept relegated to the confines of political process. This interpretation resembles the Hegelian philosophy of revolution, which proposes that revolution is a part of an evolutionary process of world historical dimensions. It was Hegel's philosophy that influenced the Marxist theory of evolution, and in turn, the Marxist theory has had great bearing on many of the revolutionary movements of this century. This dissertation will focus its attention upon works growing out of the revolutionary movements affecting change in the lives and life-styles of Afro-Americans and East Germans.

Upon first considering the Afro-American and East German experiences, one might not, perhaps, recognize any grounds for comparison. Excessive concern with racial, national, or cultural differences is apt to influence the individual to view the movements in terms of black versus white experience, or capitalist versus communist experience. This obsession with the "barriers" separating

9

the two groups tends to camouflage the fact that the racial structure of American society is very similar to, or even replication of,
the European system of social stratification. It is logical, therefore, that East Germans and black Americans experience some
very similar social problems.

This thesis - the first to compare the social development of the
contemporary Afro-American with that of his East German counterpart - analyzes works which affirm that the desire for social
justice and respect for human dignity are universals sought after
by individuals in every society. Morrison, Kant, Walker, and De
Bruyn, the authors of the works in question, share the following
three traits in common, despite the obvious differences that seemingly set them apart. First, each author champions the cause of
social development by advocating the rights of the individual. Second, each heralds self-consciousness and self-awareness as viable weapons in the battle to alleviate the social ills of alienation
and ego-obliteration. Third, each artist concentrates upon working
within his/her respective social system, despite the fact that he is
sometimes strongly critical of it. The four revolutionary artists
call for the elimination of those archaisms that decide the worth of
the human being by judging his gender, economic status, and/or
social origins rather than his individual merit. De Bruyn, Kant,
Walker, and Morrison seek to revolutionize society by depicting
characters who should help us to realize that the individual who
lacks a sense of self is doomed, regardless of his social standing.
Further, they emphasize that each of us has a moral obligation to
contribute to revolutionary movements that have the betterment of
the human condition as their goal.

Traditionally, the term revolution has called to mind scenes of
uprisings and insurrections characterized by violence. Let us clar-
ify at this point, however, that revolution and rebellion are terms
which are relative to each other rather than synonymous. If, as
both Hegel and Marx professed, revolution is evolutionary, then it
is by nature an ongoing process, continually moving toward a new
stage of development. Although certain phases of the revolutionary
process might be characterized by violent rebellion, violence is by

no means the essence of revolution. This distinction is very clearly made in the works discussed in this dissertation. The protagonist of De Bruyn's Buridians Esel, for example, cannot be classified as a revolutionary merely because he defies the authority and mores of his society; nor can the heroine of Walker's Meridian be branded a reactionary, because she refuses to participate in or condone acts of wanton and violent rebellion. The success of revolution is not determined by the degree of violence it arouses, but by the degree of positive change it brings about.

Because a sense of mutual identity and purpose is integral to any revolutionary movement, one of the aims of this dissertation is to examine the treatment of the concept of identity as a theme in the following works: Buridans Esen and Renata by Guenter De Bruyn; Die Aula by Hermann Kant; Song of Solomon, The Bluest Eye, and Sula by Toni Morrison; The Third Life of Grange Copeland and Meridian by Alice Walker. The works above were chosen because they address more than one phase of the revolutionary process, and concern themselves with themes having contemporary relevance as well as historical value. They illustrate vividly the effect of social, racial, and economic bigotry upon the development of society as a whole as well as upon that of the individual.

In order to better understand a work of art, it is necessary for the literary scholar to delve into areas that exceed the boundaries of the work itself. The biography of the author, in addition to his sources and influences, sometimes assists the student of literature in properly considering a work within its particular historical, social, and political framework.[1] The authors of the works reviewed in this dissertation all hail from working-class backgrounds, and consequently have first-hand knowledge of the worker's experience in a stratified society. For this reason, perhaps, almost all of the works are written from the point of view of the oppressed rather than the oppressor.

Although the term "images-mirages," used by the French School of Comparative Literature, generally concerns people of different national origins, it is applicable here for two reasons: (1) American blacks have historically constituted a sub-culture in this country, the image of which has been negatively projected by the dominant group, resulting in the distorted, and in many cases, aborted development of a positive self-image; (2) although East and West Germans share a common language, heritage, and culture, differing political ideologies have divided them into two distinct nations whose differences exceed those of geographical boundaries and nominal philosophies. For example, the East German's perception of the West is colored tremendously by the influence of the media, especially since foreign travel restrictions prevent most citizens from ever acquiring first-hand knowledge of the West. Subject to state censorship, East German literature tends to reinforce long-established, stereotypic preconceptions of the West. Incidentally, then, the literary image of the West affects the group-consciousness of East Germans. This is important because group consciousness is relative to the self-image of the individual.

The concept of identity, a factor integral to the understanding of the works examined in this dissertation, is an abstraction of enormous complexity involving many overlapping relationships. For example, the individual's perception of society and his position within the societal framework determine, to an extent, whether his self-image is positive or negative, and thereby ultimately affects his sense of identity. Understanding the individual requires cognizance of the society of which he is a product. Evaluation of a given society requires familiarity with, or at least awareness of, the historical events and forces which have had impact on its development. The socio-political milieu of America does not always incline favorably towards Afro-Americans or East Germans, and for this reason, the first half of this dissertation will be introduced with a review of the history of the black man in America. The latter half of the dissertation will be preceded by a review of the events that ultimately resulted in the division of Germany and the establishment of two separate German states.

To the revolutionaries of every era falls the task of correcting the ills of the past. Many critical changes have taken place in Western society as a result of World War II. The subjects of interest to this dissertation, Afro-Americans and East Germans, were affected to a greater extent than many other groups. For example, a phenomenon Ephraim Mizruchi names "declassification" explains how blacks attained positions in the government services that had been off-limits to them prior to the war.[2] On the other hand, the close of the war led to the birth of the East German nation. Such alterations would naturally have some bearing on the light in which the affected individual sees himself. Tremendous strides have been made in the areas of psychology and psychiatry, particularly those areas concerned with the concepts of identity and alienation. Although the focal point of this study is the theme of identity and its development in the novels to be examined, I will approach the topic from the standpoint of the alienated individual, for as Donald Oken writes, "allienation is the mirror of identity; the felt estrangement from one's self represents the polar opposite of knowing who one is."[3]

The nature of the literature produced in a specific nation is often determined by the reigning socio-political climate, which may also have tremendous influence upon the public response to literature and the other arts. This is evidenced by the American response to the literary creations of Afro-American feminists and East German socialists, who have been given proper consideration only in the last few years. Often the victims of double discrimination, black feminists usually devote much of their writing to issues that mainstream Americans view in an unfavorable light. This disfavor manifests itself in the lack of critical materials treating the works of authors like Morrison and Walker. Naturally, this has great bearing upon literary studies that concern themselves with the works of such authors. Polemical political systems, long-time hindrances to cultural exchange between the United States and the German Democratic Republic, have left their scars in the areas of literary exchange especially. For example, there is presently no direct line of copyright ties between the two nations. Relatively few American-authored critical works are devoted to the study of East German literature, and finally, only a minimal number of East German-authored works have been translated into English (and most of those translations tend to be second rate). This indicates that the political milieus of both nations contribute to limiting the accessibility of East German writings to the American public.

The examination of individual self-consciousness (or the lack of it) is the central theme of every work analyzed in this dissertation. Morrison and Walker achieve their ends by third-person narrative, while Kant and De Bruyn approach their goals by stream-of-consciousness. Each author requires the reader to journey back and forth from the realm of the past to that of the present. These spiritual odysseys are necessary if the reader is to comprehend fully the stages of development each character experiences, and how the self-image of each is affected. To understand who the character is, and who he ultimately becomes, one must first know who he has been. To know at which point he has arrived in life, and where he intends to go, one must know from whence he came. As Hermann Kant writes in the opening lines of Die Aula: "Man konnte keine Zukunft haben ohne Vergangenheit."[4] As they allow us to plunge into the psyches of their characters, Morrison, Walker, Kant, and De Bruyn advise us of the importance of knowing ourselves.

Notes

[1] Beverly Harris-Schenz, "Images of the Black in Eighteenth Century Literature," Stanford University, 1977, p. 4.
[2] Ephraim H. Mizruchi, "An Introduction to the Notion of Alienation," in Alienation: Concept, Term, and Meanings, ed. Frank Johnson (New York: Seminar Press, 1973), pp. 111-24.
[3] Donald Oken, "Alienation and Identity: Some Comments on Adolescence, the Counterculture and Contemporary Adaptations," in Alienation: Concept, Term, and Meanings, ed. Frank Johnson (New York: Seminar Press, 1973), pp. 83-110.
[4] Hermann Kant, Die Aula, (Berlin: Rutten & Loening, 1966), p. 9.

Chapter 1

AFRO-AMERICAN LITERARY IMAGES

Alienation has been a dominant factor of the black experience in America almost from the time of the European discovery. Although the first blacks to land on America's shores were not slaves but free men more familiar with the cultures of Europe than those of Africa (they were the black explorers who sailed with Columbus), the earliest extant samples of black literature were written by blacks who had felt the yoke of slavery, and therefore reflect the slave mentality and an acceptance of the images and symbols of degradation used to describe blacks in white literature.[1] Later works by black authors, such as Clotel or the President's Daughter by William Wells Brown (1815-1884), reflect a strong desire on the part of blacks for total assimilation into the mainstream of American, i.e., white, society. Even prior to the introduction of formal black slavery in America, the black man, presumably because of cultural and physical differences, was not easily - and never fully - assimilated into the mainstream of American society. The establishment of black slavery as an American institution further widened the gap dividing whites and blacks. The view developed that blacks were not merely different from whites, but inferior to them. This "inherent" inferiority, as it were, constituted a major justification for the system of slavery. If one were to "reconstruct the major episodes in the history of American race relations," as Eli Ginzberg and Alfred Eichner suggest, one would have to conclude that blacks, whether free or enslaved, have always been "outsiders" in American society.[2] The fact that he was black, and therefore visibly different from and presumably inferior to the vast majority of the population was a factor used to justify the enslavement of the black man for centuries. Slavery, the cheapest form of labor, was necessary to maintain the economic standard America enjoyed; the black presence was necessary for the maintenance of slavery; therefore, the black presence was tolerated in America as long as it was contained within the boundaries of slavery or relegated to a level of inferior status. Ginzberg and Eichner cite examples of noted historical figures, who firmly supported this belief. They quote from a speech of Abraham Lincoln, traditionally seen as a champion of freedom for the black man, wherein Lincoln eulogized Henry Clay for seeking to remove the "troublesome presence of free Negroes" from American shores.[3] The abolition of slavery did little to change the relationship between the black man and American society. Granted his freedom, but not prepared or trained properly to utilize it to his fullest advantage, the black man still found white society closed to him. Blacks were further handicapped by the lack of a strong sense of national identity. The unifying factors, i.e., the sources of psychological sustenance which normally bind a people together - family ties, language, religion, and culture - had been obliterated by the particular brand of slavery existing in the United States. Educationally and socially deprived, with no means of political redress, and suffering from a constantly reinforced sense of inferiority, the American black remained alienated from the mainstream of the society in which he had been born.

While not the primary topic of this study, bigotry is of primary importance to it, because of its overall effects on society in general. Because racism is so deeply rooted in the historical tradition of America, it is often reflected in literature. The appearance of blacks in American literature dates back to the colonial period. Seldom, if ever, portrayed as a serious or mature character, the black was usually depicted as the stereotypic buffoon, the lazy prankster, the docile slave, or the treacherous, surly servant. Sterling Brown makes the following observation:

> Treatment of the Negro in American fiction, since it parallels his treatment in American life, has naturally been noted for its injustice. Like other oppressed and exploited minorities, the Negro has been interpreted in a way to justify his exploiters.[4]

Having no other models, early black American writers patterned their works after those of Europeans and white Americans. Addison Gayle, Jr. charges that

> Early black writers did not attempt to re-create legends of the past, create symbols, images or metaphors anew, nor

provide literary vehicles by which men, out of the marrow
of suffering, might be redeemed in myth if not actuality;
instead, they either accepted the propaganda of their detrac-
tors, or burned their talents into ashes in attempts to refuse them.[5]

Gayle's accusation is true, but it does not take into consideration
a very important factor, namely, that since knowledge of the distant past and his African origins were transmitted to the black man
via the dominant, white, racist culture, which considered Africa a
land of horror, where emotion prevailed over reason, the black
man's image of his distant past was a negative one. He viewed his
more recent past as a time of ignominy rather than glory; therefore, to rise above what he perceived as the humiliation of the
past, his own past, he chose to ignore or reject it and adopt a
European surrogate in its place. Marion Berghahn refers to this
as the rejection of the "African Ego," the psychologically destructive repercussions of which play a central role in Afro-American
life and literature to this day.[6] Employing his/her art as a medium,
the revolutionary artist addresses the task of resolving the social
and psychological ills that have grown out of these conditions.

Throughout the ages, art has occupied a significant place in every
society, and often the artist plays a viable role in revolutionizing
society. Recognizing that they could indeed constitute a powerful
weapon, Plato, in his Republic, counseled keeping the arts subject to state censorship and control. The founding fathers of the
German Democratic Republic were no doubt in agreement with
Plato, since steps were taken to establish an official national ideology which brought the arts in East Germany under the control of
the state four years prior to the official founding of that nation.
Hans-Dietrich Sander states, "Die SED begann mit der Planung
der Literatur noch bevor die DDR gegruendet wurde ... Am 8.
August 1945 wurde der Kulturbund gegruendet."[7] Unlike the East
Germans, American black nationalists lacked the political power
to enact and/or enforce a law capable of harnessing the force of
the arts to suit their specific needs. Nevertheless, literature and
the arts were recognized as powerful expressions of human ex-

perience, and therefore, ideological weapons of tremendous magnitude. The arts were successfully utilized during the Black Awareness and Black Power Movements of the 1960s and early 1970s. In fact, statements by black nationalists echo those of DDR spokesmen. Ron Karenga advocates, "Black art, like everything else in the black community, must respond to the reality of revolution. It must become and remain a part of the revolutionary machinery. ..."[8] Otto Grotewahl, former Ministaerpraesident of the German Democratic Republic, voices the same sentiments: "Literatur und bildende Kuenste sind der Politik untergeordnet, aber es ist klar, dass sie einen starken Einfluss auf die Politik ausueben." (31 August 1951)[9]

Since the time of the ancients, critics have acknowledged that every artist sustains a dual relationship: one with his/her art and another with society. This is particularly true of the revolutionary artist, whose duty is to "respond to the reality of revolution" by promoting change for the common good via his/her art. The revolutionary artist is successful only if his/her work reflects an understanding of the balanced relationship between the historical nature and the social function of art. While communication is the goal of all art forms, revolutionary art must celebrate positive images that serve an instructional purpose, that is to say, revolutionary art by its very nature is didactic. This fact often sets the revolutionary and the formalist values at odds. The former perceives the notion of art for art's sake as totally decadent; the latter may tolerate didacticism as an acceptable aspect of literature up to a point, but generally regards it in a derogatory light, arguing that it subverts the object of art to lesser and ignoble purposes. Since he is influenced by traditional and revolutionary philosophies, the revolutionary artist must surmount a number of paradoxical situations to successfully satisfy his moral obligation to teach and enlighten. To create art which is genuine, he must be able to ferret out that which is artificial. He must ever create anew, while simultaneously preserving that which was created before his time. He must see everything with fresh eyes and re-create true to life. He is also required to be able to distinguish the genuine art of revolution from the reactionary and superficial. He must hold himself slightly aloof from society, while involving himself in social affairs; that is to say, the artist is the conscience and voice of the people, but he also is the people.[10] He recognizes that life is constantly changing and that he must also be open to change if he is to become the most complete person he possibly can be.

We see these tenets exemplified first in the works of Toni Morrison and Alice Walker. Like many other black writers, Morrison and Walker protest the atrocities of racism by centering their themes around the ignominies and horrors of racist society, which impede, cripple, or altogether prevent the proper development of human relationships. Unlike many of their predecessors or contemporaries, however, neither Morrison nor Walker is overly concerned or preoccupied with "the man," i.e., the term with which black American dialect refers to white racist society. Unlike the black apologetic writers, they do not write to educate the white public about black life, or to convince whites that "blacks are people, too." They do not, after the fashion of the apocalyptic writers, admonish white America about the evils of racism; nor do they threaten white America with an ensuing "Armaggedon" if social injustices go unrequited. Morrison and Walker are concerned with depicting the effects of racism insofar as they affect the development of the self-image of the individual, and consequently, the interpersonal relationships of the individual with others. They are concerned with pointing out to the individual, the black individual in particular, that each person is obligated to strive toward the most positive and complete level of self-development possible, despite the fact that the negative images projected by a racist society have been and continue to be psychologically impairing. Although they depict the harsh realities of black life, the works of Morrison and Walker, in Morrison's own words, "bear witness that centuries of brutalization have not created a race of brutes." By concentrating upon self-awareness, self-development, self-love and self-acceptance, the individual will survive, because he will manage to protect his inner being from destructive external forces. In the following lines from an essay about blacks, images, and image makers, Mary Helen Washington agrees with the sentiments of Morrison and

Walker that, "Constant looking backward only keeps us attentive to what the "man" writes about us. Problems are solved by moving ahead. ... Images have power to shape and control our lives. Which images shall we choose to celebrate?"[11]

The roots of art are deeply embedded in the personal experience of the artist, for one best recreates that which is intimately familiar. Written from a pointedly feminist perspective, The Bluest Eye (1970), Sula (1973) and Song of Solomon (1977) span a period of roughly forty years, from the 1920s to the 1960s. Depicted in these novels are scenes from black life, as experienced in the small towns of the Midwest. The small town settings are patterned after Morrison's own hometown of Lorain, Ohio, where she was born in 1931.

In an interview with Robert B. Steptoe, Morrison explains why she took particular pains to create a strong sense of "community" in her works, especially the last two novels:

> My tendency is to focus on neighborhoods and communities. The community, the black community ... was always there, only we called it the "neighborhood." And there was this life-giving, very, very strong sustenance that people got from the neighborhood. One lives, really, not so much in your house as you do outside of it. ... Legal responsibilities, all the responsibilities that agencies now have were the responsibilities of the neighborhood.[12]

She obviously considers the neighborhood or community a very powerful component in identity development.

In addition to discussing the role of the community in her works, Morrison points out that two of the novels are set in her native Ohio, because that state is interesting from the historic point of view of black people.[13] To the north, Ohio is bordered by Canada, the ultimate destination of the Underground Railroad, while to the south lies Kentucky, the last stronghold of slavery encountered before the fugitive slave crossed the Ohio River to freedom. The home of ardent Abolitionists and the Ku Klux Klan, Ohio symbolizes a synthesis of North and South. Morrison's characters re-enact the experiences of blacks who reside in small Northern towns, but have not, for the most part, lost ties with their Southern heritage. Morrison bears witness (as a black revolutionary artist) to the resiliency, courage, and heroism of those blacks who grew up under enormous economic duress, yet never were degraded by it. To quote from her interview with Bandler,

> We bear witness and reveal that world, and that life, and those people, not in the perfection and heroism alone, but also in the ugliness. Then one can sift, take out the experiences that can be valuable, and move to the next step.[14]

Each human being must engage in some form of struggle if he is to develop an identity of his own. The struggle of black Americans toward a positive self-image has been particularly difficult in the face of past historical injuries and injustices and today's persisting vestiges of racism. There is no form of slavery which does not offend nature and man, but the particular brand of slavery practiced in North America until the middle of the nineteenth century proved monstrously detrimental to the psyche of black Americans. Not only did slavery sanction the bondage of a particular group of human beings; it also sought to perpetuate itself by denying their "personhood" or human status. As mentioned earlier, the practice of disallowing the use of African languages, forbidding the practice of African religions, and the deliberate separation of members of the same tribe did much to dispel the chances for blacks to develop a strong sense of national identity during the years of slavery. More detrimental, in my opinion, than any of those practices was the custom of separating families, which resulted in the disintegration of the family unit among a sizable percentage of blacks, and/or the establishment of the system of black matriarchy. More than a century after slavery ceased to be an active institution in the United States, the psychology of slavery remains deeply embedded in the American consciousness. To a great extent, this can be attributed to the fact that many of the conditions existing prior to the abolition of slavery were not altered following the close of the Civil War. Blacks were faced not only with the problems of reversing the negative effects of centuries of bondage, but also with those of preventing the reinforcement of those same ills among their numbers. This proved to be a slow, tedious process. As blacks struggled to conform to economic and cultural standards that were not designed for them, they often endured frustrations and tribulations that took their toll on black family unity and stability. In each of her novels, Morrison portrays aspects of black family life on various social and economic levels, all of which show evidence of the influence of oppression. While she does not spare her reader from exposure to the ugliness and evils of life, she rejects the false and dehumanizing images projected by the system, and celebrates the rediscovery, acceptance, and development of the "self." If E. Franklin Frazier is correct in his assumption that the lack of a social organization to sustain the black man's African heritage in America has affected black identity development - group and national identity in particular - then what can one expect of the individual who has never known the support and protection of the most basic social organization, the stable family! [15] If the family does not reinforce the individual's belief in his own positive self-image during the formative years, how does he learn to become self-assertive? Denied the psychological support of his family, how does the individual learn to sustain himself? Morrison suggests a solution that is very simple, although it might not be easy. Once the individual learns to properly love himself, he finds it easier to love his brother, and once black people learn to sustain each other in mutual love, many of the questions which appear above will be answered.

Notes

[1]Addison Gayle, Jr., The Way of the New World: The Black Novel in America (Garden City, New York: Anchor Press/Doubleday, 1975), p. 19.

[2]Eli Ginzberg and Alfred S. Eichner, The Troublesome Presence (New York: Mentor Books, 1964), p. 13.

[3]Ginzberg and Eichner, pp. 14-15.

[4]Sterling Brown, The Negro in American Fiction (Albany: J. B. Lyon, 1937), p. 64.

[5]Gayle, p.xiii.

[6]Marion Berghahn, Images of Black Africa in Black American Literature (London: Macmillan, 1977), p.23.

[7]Hans-Dietrich Sander, Geschichte der schoenen Literatur in der DDR (Freiburg: Rombach, 1972), p.209.

[8]Ron Karenga, "Black Cultural Nationalism," in The Black Aesthetic , ed., Addison Gayle, Jr. (Garden City, New York: Anchor Books/Doubleday, 1972), p.209.

[9]Elimar Schubbe, ed., Dokumente zur Kunst-Literatur- und Kulturpolitik in der SED, 1965-1971 (Stuttgart: n.p., 1972), p.209.

[10]Alice Walker, "The Unglamorous but Worthwhile Duties of the Black Revolutionary Artist or ... of the Black Writer Who Simply Works and Writes," Black Collegian, Sept.-Oct. 1971, p.43.

[11]Mary Helen Washington, "Black Women Image Makers," Black World, Aug. 1972, n. pag.

[12]Michael S. Harper and Robert B. Stepto, eds., "Intimate Things in Place: A Conversation with Toni Morrison," in Chant of Saints (Chicago: University of Illinois Press, 1979), p.214.

[13]Harper and Stepto, p.215.

[14]Michael J. Bandler, "Novelist Toni Morrison: 'We Bear Witness," African Woman, Sept.-Oct. 1979, p.28.

[15]E. Franklin Frazier, The Negro Family in the United States (New York: Dryden Press, 1948), p.17.

Chapter 2

THE BLUEST EYE: THE AMERICAN DREAM VS.
BLACK SELF-CONCEPT

The black experience in America has historically been the antithesis of the American Dream. Toni Morrison approaches the struggle for identity in The Bluest Eye on the level of antithesis: black/
white, male/female, parent/child, morality/immorality. The myth
of the American Dream has long professed that success awaits the
rugged individual industrious enough to carve for himself a niche
in society. Such a myth necessarily fosters a strong competitive
spirit in a society which measures one's degree of personal success in terms of social status, material wealth, and personal
achievement. Only a minute percentage of the American population has found the Protestant work ethic totally effective in guaran-
teeing success. It is those few, however, who become the trend-
setters or the "significant others" for the rest of the nation. It is
from those significant few, as it were, that we acquire identity.
We become obsessed with assuming the roles society assigns us,
and instead of concentrating on our inner being, we concentrate on
our objective image, evaluating ourselves and validating our identity through the evaluation of significant others.[1] Historically, this
has been a tragic situation for the black American, who has found
it very difficult to establish group or self-identity of social value
comparable to that of the Anglo-Saxon majority. If the ideal image
projected by society is synonymous with white middle class values,
only imitations or distorted replicas of that image can be expected
from a group whose own positive self-image has been mutilated by
the dominant group, and which remains practically powerless to
create positive images anew. The Bluest Eye opens with an example of just such a syndrome. The first paragraph describe the "typical" (white) American family, consisting of both parents, two children, a dog and a cat, contentedly enjoying each other's company
and the beauty of their home. Directly below appear fourteen "lines"
composed of exactly the same words as the paragraph above, but

totally without form and punctuation. Because they are not capital-
ized, the proper nouns lose all sense of distinction in their relationship to the other nouns in the "sentence." Persons are not dis-
tinguishable from objects, one word is not distinct from the one
which precedes it, nor from the one which follows it. The image
itself is distorted and disturbing, because nothing described has
any form or meaning. This image, then, symbolizes the distortion
in the human lives to be portrayed in the novel.

Identity is a major concern of black and white Americans alike.
The black must constantly assert himself to establish a positive
image, while the white seeks to maintain his image of superiority
by maintaining the status quo, which is founded upon the myth of
black inferiority. Morrison assumes that the reader is knowledgeable in the area of race relations. We should remember that she
writes primarily to enlighten the black audience, which would, of
course, be knowledgeable about its own experiences and history.
She does not, therefore, deem it necessary to make many overt
references to the racial situation. A covert, but fervent strain of
polemical bias can be perceived, but the guilt of institutional racism
is implied rather than stated in a straight-forward manner. Nevertheless, the reader knows in no uncertain terms that it - institutional racism - has been and continues to be a formidable obstacle
in the lives of America's black citizens.

After the fashion of the "messenger" in a Greek tragedy, Claudia,
the narrator, opens with a monologue and sets the stage for the
scenes to follow. Her account of events and dates creates strong
impressions of place and time, enabling the reader to establish an
historic perspective by recalling events which occurred outside the
community of the novel, but which had bearing on the lives of those
who lived within. Using images of fertility and barrenness, and the
metaphor of dissemination, Claudia creates a mood of futility and
guilt, of helplessness and unnaturalness, meaningful not only within
the context of The Bluest Eye, but generally applicable to the black
experience in America:

> It was a long time before my sister and I admitted to ourselves
> that no green was going to spring from our seeds. Once we

knew, our guilt was relieved only by fights and mutual accusations about who was to blame. For years I thought my sister was right: it was my fault. ... It never occurred to either of us that the earth itself might have been unyielding.[2]

Barrenness may result from a diseased or infertile receptacle – whatever the receptacle might be - as well as from dead seeds or improper sowing. At another point, she makes a brief and simple statement, which addresses itself to the human experience:

A little examination and much less melancholy would have proved to us that our seeds were not the only ones that did not sprout; nobody's did. Not even the gardens fronting the lake showed marigolds that year. (p. 9)

The guilt and melancholy whereof the narrator speaks are symbolic of the emotions many black youth are socialized to feel, because they often appear to fall short of the norm or the accepted ideal. In the case of Claudia and her sister, however, if barrenness or retarded growth were a sign of guilt or inadequacy, then those shortcomings were experienced collectively by all who resided in their town. Morrison notes that the unfruitfulness afflicted the white and the black, the wealthy and the poor neighborhoods alike. With those two sentences, Morrison, through Claudia, gives voice to the realization that affliction is reality common to all human beings, regardless of race, sex, or economic bracket. As soon as the individual arrives at this realization, he finds it easier to achieve the self-acceptance and self-love necessary for human development. Our narrator, who happens to be a child a few years younger than the protagonist, closes the monologue, committing herself to the task of giving an account of the events which take place within the novel. Claudia claims that explaining why things happened as they did would be beyond her ability, so she devotes her efforts to relating how things happened. Perhaps Morrison is suggesting that each reader would benefit more if he were to analyze the situation using his own frame of reference.

Briefly, The Bluest Eye is an account of a young black girl, Pecola Breedlove, who believes the ugliness and brutality she encounters in her daily life derive from what she conceives of as her own personal ugliness. She is convinced that she can eliminate the problems by eradicating, or at least camouflaging her handicap behind the skyblue eyes of a white girl. The tragic circumstances examined in The Bluest Eye are not merely the personal tragedies of Pecola - they are the tragedies of generations of others, who like the Breedloves, were indoctrinated with the conviction that they were the most contemptible of human beings. The author focuses her attention primarily on the thoughts and actions of Claudia and her sister, Frieda, rather than those of Pecola, who longs for the blue eyes mentioned in the title. There is a possible explanation for this. The examination of the character and her actions discloses that Pecola is actually a type of stock character, used by Morrison to personify total subjugation. The reader must always bear in mind that the revolutionary author has an obligation to create positive images, that revolutionary art must contain an element of didacticism. Pecola is the kind of character who might arouse the reader's sympathy, but she represents nothing positive or affirmative. She cannot, therefore, be celebrated as a model of revolutionary development. Her great tragedy is having been born into a situation of psychological and spiritual stagnation that aborted her individual development. For this reason, she has no control over the direction of her own life; nor can she entertain any hope of ever being able to exercise any such control. This, for Toni Morrison, is an anathema. Although she is sympathetic to the pain and suffering she endures, the author nevertheless consigns Pecola to the realm of madness, and dooms her to a state of barrenness (unproductiveness), symbolized by the death of her baby. She is isolated, so to speak, to prevent the further spread of the particular "disease" she carries. Pecola is somewhat reminiscent of Kafka's Gregor Samsa. Both Gregor and Pecola suffer from a tremendous sense of guilt, which is not of their own making, but prompts them to submit passively to the psychotic mangling of the personality, the damage from which is irreversible. Gregor, by not protesting such treatment, condemns himself to remain a dung beetle. Pecola receives the blue eyes of her dreams, but relinquishes her soul in return for them.

The source of Pecola's malady can be traced back to the childhood of her parents. Neither Cholly nor Pauline had grown up in an atmosphere conducive to positive self-affirmation. Neither parent could provide the child the means for a sense of self-assurance they themselves had never attained.

Acute alienation had plagued Pauline since early childhood, driving her to seek relief in fantasy, as most people do at some point in life. For Pauline, however, fantasizing becomes a crutch she cannot relinquish. She develops such a sophisticated technique of indulging herself in fantasy that she becomes adept at finding love images even in spirituals and other religious hymns. Pauline falls in love with her husband, not because of who he is, but because he is the first man to give form to her fantasy of a lover. Her excessive indulgence in fantasy grows to such an extent as to be judged decadent by the author. Like Thomas Mann in <u>Budden-brooks</u>, Morrison manifests that decadence with the symbol of decaying teeth. (Pauline loses the first tooth while engrossed in a Jean Harlow movie.) Morrison believes Pauline bears a greater share of the responsibility for what happens to Pecola at her father's hands than even Cholly himself.

The forerunner of Morrison's "golden-eyed, free characters," Cholly Breedlove is a man bound by no ties of convention. A free spirit, he acts in accordance with his own impulses and desires only. Ironically enough, even his name suggests something of the unconventional and the animalistic. Yellow eyes symbolize Cholly's freedom of spirit. (That same feature is shared by characters in subsequent Morrison novels: Sula, for example, has goldflecked eyes[3] and her lover, Ajax, yellow eyes; Guitar Baines is described as having "cat eyes resembling gashes of gold."[4])

Deserted by both parents in infancy, Cholly is reared by an elderly aunt, who dies when he is thirteen, leaving him "abandoned" once again. What little he knows of love, he learns from Aunt Jimmy, whose world is strictly female, marked by folkloric tradition and populated by dowagers as ancient as herself. His first relationship with a female in his own age group is sexual in nature and ends with his introduction to bitter hatred and humiliation. That experience is also the first occasion of his later habit of laying the guilt for his own shortcomings at the door of another: "For now, he hated the one who bore witness to his failure, his impotence, the one whom he had not been able to protect, to spare, to cover from the round moon glow of the flashlight. " (p. 119)

Aunt Jimmy's death leaves him "free" to do what he likes, bound by nothing and no one: "Abandoned in a junk heap by his mother, rejected for a crap game by his father, there was nothing more to lose. He was alone with his own perceptions and appetites, and they alone interested him. " (p. 126)

Marriage, in the traditional sense, is not an institution intended for a man like Cholly; and marriage to a woman trying to live in accordance with a prescribed master plan is especially unbearable. Inept in the role of husband, he is worse in that of father. Whereas Cholly is the victim of his passions, his children are the victims of their father:

> Having no idea of how to raise children, and having never watched any parent raise himself, he could not even comprehend what such a relationship should be. . . Had he not been alone in the world since he was thirteen knowing only a dying old woman who felt responsible for him, but whose age, sex, and interests were so remote from his own, he might have felt a stable connection between himself and the children. As it was, he reacted to them, and his reactions were based on what he felt at the moment. (pp. 126-127)

Her many descriptions of the interactions of mother and child, e. g., Pilate with Hagar, Pilate with Reba, Reba with Hagar, Ruth with Milkman, Helene with Nel, etc., suggest that Morrison sees a spiritual quality in that relationship. Although Cholly is in no way exonerated for his part in bringing about Pecola's collapse, Morrison appears to point to Pauline as the parent who fails her daughter in the most crucial matters. Pauline's obsession with physical beauty has made her aware that she herself is not beautiful according to Anglo-European standards. Her children, therefore, are also not beautiful in her eyes, for Morrison writes that she taught them to "wear their ugliness, put it on, so to speak, although it did not belong to them. " (p. 34) That her own sense of inadequacy and frustration would prevent any mother from recognizing the beauty of her own baby is both shocking and heartbreaking: "A right smart baby she was. I used to like to watch her. You know, they makes them greedy sounds. Eyes all soft and wet ... But I knowed she was ugly. Head full of pretty hair, but Lord she was ugly." (pp. 99-100) Ironically enough, Pauline gives the baby the name of a "beautiful" mulatto character in a movie she sees – Pecola or sheep face. This makes one pause and wonder about her standards of beauty. Of course, her daughter resembles the fair-skinned girl in no way. This obsession with the image of the white child is mirrored in Pecola's fascination with Shirley Temple, the blond, blue-eyed child-star of the 1930s and 1940s. Pecola is so taken with Shirley that she manages to drink three quarts of milk just for the chance to contemplate Shirley's picture, imprinted on her cup. Pauline's rejection of Pecola's ugliness (her own ugliness) results in her failing the child in a number of ways. She neglects to initiate Pecola into the mysteries of womanhood, and the task falls to Frieda, who is even younger than Pecola! She demonstrates no affection for her, going so far as to beat and berate her own child, while comforting and petting her white charge. The ultimate outrage is the physical attack Pauline launches on Pecola in a fit of jealous rage, upon learning that the girl has been raped. In violating his daughter's body, Cholly sins against man and nature, but such gross neglect and cruelty by the mother, the transmitter of culture and life, who destroys her child's soul in addition to battering her body, proves perhaps far more devastating.

Yet as mentioned earlier, the narrator, Claudia, is far more visible in the novel than the supposed protagonist. She highlights the characteristics of Pecola because she is the elder girl's opposite. Through Claudia's eyes, the reader becomes familiar with her own family, the MacTeers, and is apprised of all the hardships and pressures which confront them and every other black family not belonging to the more privileged, professional class. From the information provided by Claudia, the reader discerns that The Bluest Eye opens in the autumn of 1940. The sequence of events follows from that time to the autumn of the following year. It is through Claudia's eyes, in short, that the reader sees the novel in perspective.

For the average black, the years following the Depression were
financially precarious and improved only after the beginning of
World War II. Blacks, with the exception of a privileged few, did
not partake of the general affluence the rest of the nation enjoyed.
In Northern urban areas, they occupied substandard housing,
worked at the least desirable jobs, and lived with the knowledge
that they were the most expendable component of the labor force.
Want and deprivation threatened constantly, and uncertainty was
a way of life. Andrew Billingsley describes the situation thus:

> The dramatically increased economic hazards faced by the
> Negro ethnic subsociety, and the consequences of the caste
> system have a direct bearing on the difficulty and complexity
> of carrying out the major instrumental functions of the Ne-
> gro family. The white breadwinner's security of employment
> and his reliance upon community systems in fulfilling the
> functions of providing stability and basic needs to family
> members are denied the Negro breadwinner.[5]

Perhaps it was their poverty of spirit which set the Breedloves
apart from their neighbors and each other; but their financial and
material misfortunes were in no way unique. During World War I
and the years that followed, millions of blacks fled the South - a
phneomenon known as the Great Migration - seeking employment
in Northern factories, and a better standard of living. Most of
them did not find the North the promised land of their expectations.
The Breedloves and the MacTeers were two such families.

By comparing the two families, Morrison uses each to define the
other in terms of contrast, although they appear to have many
superficial similarities. Each family, for example, is comprised
of four members, two children and two parents. In the case of
both families, the mother is required to work, and the two income
brackets are comparable. The Breedloves shoulder no more responsibility than the MacTeers; yet unstable familial relations
cause them to meet their obligations in a drastically different
manner. Claudia and Frieda are not strangers to harshness, poverty, or ugliness any more than Pecola, as is implied by such episodes as the confrontations with their mother, the reference to

collecting coal and taking in a roomer to augment the family income, or with the vivid description of their house, with its human and non-human residents. Poverty and all that accompanies it is part of their lives, but they are never degraded by it, owing to the pride and individuality each girl feels. Pecola, on the other hand, does fall prey to the ravages of spiritual poverty, because she goes totally lacking in the area of positive self-conception. The MacTeer girls move with confidence unknown to the Breedlove child. One's conception of oneself is reflected in the manner in which one reacts to external forces. For example, both Frieda and Pecola admire the beauty of Shirley Temple, America's golden girl. Pecola, however, interprets Shirley's comeliness as a highlight of her own ugliness, a denial of her beauty; Frieda, on the other hand, sees it as a beauty different from her own, but in no way superior. Frieda and Claudia confront and often reject the values of the white world. Pecola shrinks from them in shame. Claudia's reaction to the attempts at forcing those social values on her are often violent in nature and are manifested in her destruction of white baby dolls and her burning hatred of Shirley Temple: "... I hated Shirley, not because she was cute, but because she danced with Bojangles, who was my friend, my uncle, my daddy. " (p. 19) The egocentricity of childhood causes Claudia to reject that which is alien and threatening to her. Rejection of herself, however, stimulates acute anger toward those who reject her, because the pride and sense of "uniqueness of self" instilled by her parents enable her to vent her anger by directing it without rather than within.

As a revolutionary writer, Morrison is concerned with survival: who survives and why.[6] From the outset, the reader knows that the MacTeer girls survive and Pecola does not. Ample information about the past history of Pauline and Cholly Breedlove is provided in an attempt to explain the demise of their family. What is known about the MacTeer parents is learned directly from the narrator, or deduced from an analysis of the behavior of their children, since children, to a great extent, reflect the values and beliefs of their parents. Trager and Yarrow emphasize:

The child's need for acceptance by persons important to him ... his conformity to their patterns of behavior and attitude. Deviations from the patterns of behavior and beliefs of his family and group may result in frustration of his needs to be accepted and to belong. Attitudes towards self and toward others are acquired in this process of attempting to secure needed satisfaction and to obtain meaning from the confusion of stimuli affecting the individual.[7]

Pecola bowed to the same fate that engulfed her parents, i.e., accepting the image of herself that was projected by white racist society, and assuming a role accordingly, without ever realizing that the image itself was false, based upon negative myth. Self-assertion depends upon the willingness of the individual to create new values and meanings based upon the inalterable components of past experience. Her desire for blue eyes indicates a desire on Pecola's part to transcend reality without having to confront it. The futility of such a desire is expressed in Soaphead Church's letter to God, and represented in the pathetic image of the mad Pecola as she mimics the winging of a bird.

A certain imaginative egocentricity and strong-willed individuality emanate from the MacTeers, while the Breedlove personality seems to be blanketed in an aura of silent brooding and tense terror. The reader tends to think of the two families and households in terms of the Romantic contrasted with a Gothic counterpart. The behavior of Claudia and Frieda as opposed to Pecola's suggests that Morrison believes in self-determination rather than determinism. Despite the introduction of elements which bespeak the Romantic and Gothic traditions, a balance between human responsibility and the chance workings of fate is always maintained. In the narrator's monologue, the author introduces the theme of the "fall", i.e., the loss of innocence, and suggests that the acquisition of knowledge of self and love is most important, for only through this can one realize that the existence of racism does not validate it. Those who refuse to be destroyed by a lie, such as Claudia and Frieda, are far stronger than the perpetrators of that lie.

Notes

[1]Lou Benson, <u>Images, Heroes, and Self-Perceptions: the Struggle for Identity, From Mask-Wearing to Authenticity</u> (Englewood Cliffs, N. J.: Prentice-Hall, 1974), p. 4.

[2]Toni Morrison, <u>The Bluest Eye</u> (New York: Holt, Rinehart, and Winston, 1970), p. 9. All quotations will be from this edition.

[3]Toni Morrison, <u>Sula</u> (New York: Alfred A. Knopf, 1973), p. 45.

[4]Toni Morrison, <u>Song of Solomon</u> (New York: Alfred A. Knopf, 1977), p. 22.

[5]Andrew Billingsley, <u>Black Families in White America</u> (Englewood Cliffs: Prentice-Hall, 1968), p. 25.

[6]Helen G. Trager and Marian Radke Yarrow, <u>They Learn What They Live</u> (New York: Harper, 1952), p. 115.

Chapter 3

SULA: RACISM, SEXISM, AND BLACK IDENTITY

> The slave may be freed and woman be where she is, but
> woman cannot be freed and the slave remain where he is.[1]

Contemporary feminist Shulamith Firestone opens chapter five of
her work, The Dialectic of Sex, with the above lines - excerpts
from a letter written by pioneer abolitionist-feminist, Theodore
Weld. An appropriate prelude to the chapter entitled "Racism: The
Sexism of the Family of Man," this aphorism is very significant
(even as early as the beginning of the nineteenth century), because
it discloses the fact that progressive thinkers had come to recognize parallels in the status of blacks and women in America (insofar as each group comprises a political minority, subject to the
authority of the patriarchal, white, male majority).

The latter half of that century saw Friedrich Engels challenge the
legitimacy of the patriarchal family organizarion in a theoretical
treatise. Greatly influenced by the works of Johann Bachofen (Das
Mutterrecht) and Louis Morgan (Ancient Society), Engels' treatise,
Der Ursprung der Familie, des Privateigentums und des Staats
(1884) advances the theory that the origin of the concept of property can be traced to the subjugation and ownership of women, a
characteristic inherently related to patriarchy, and was accom-
panied by other ills deplored by Engels: the ownership of persons
(beginning with women and progressing to other forms of slavery);
the institution of class, caste, rank, and ruling and propertied
classes; the steady development of unequally distributed wealth;
and finally, the state.[2]

Regardless of the fact that theorists have long been aware of the
similar difficulties faced by blacks and women, because of their
minority status, very little serious attention has been directed
toward finding a solution for the problem. Even though historical
events have called attention to the existence of a double standard

in American society, which discriminates on the basis of race and sex, only a handful of sociologists have addressed the dilemma in a meaningful manner.[3] Kate Millett has listed Gunnar Myrdal, Helen Mayer Hacker, and Marlene Dixon as sociologists whose comparisons of attributes commonly ascribed to women and blacks reveal that general opinion often associates the same traits to both groups, e.g., contentment with their lot in life; inferior intelligence; primitive, childlike emotions, etc.[4] Like the relationship between the races in America, that between the sexes is also described as a situation of majority versus minority, wherein discriminatory, exploitative practices prevail.[5] It stands to reason, therefore, that the ego-destructive relationship of dominance and subordination, which generally mars the psyche-development of American Blacks, would also be psychologically harmful to women, and have double repercussions for black women, who suffer both racial and sexual oppression. For this reason, women were among the most ardent of the revolutionaries protesting the improprieties of the American social and political system during the 1960's and 1970's.

Ironically, though not surprisingly, women were relegated to positions of secondary importance within the hierarchy of the revolutionary coalition. Males dominated in the formulation of basic premises, the writing of manifestos, and the devising of strategy and tactics. Females were generally consigned to making coffee, typing, and providing sexual gratification for the males.[6] Yet it was the action of a woman, Rosa Parks, that sparked the first act of unified black protest in the Civil Rights Movement in 1955.[7] Even though the Black Power Movement advocated the right of all black people to define their own futures, it became evident in the early stages of the movement that the equality, freedom, and opportunity proclaimed by the revolution were readily available to the male contingent only. The movement afforded the black man the opportunity to flaunt his "manhood," which in American society is always associated with power and dominance, before the eyes of the white man.[8] True products of the Western patriarchal society, a considerable number of black males chose the subjugation of the black female as an effective means of assertion, believing such behavior would put them on equal par with the white man, who had, over the years, subjected the white woman to his authority. (This is evidenced by the roles assigned to women in the male-authored black plays that emerged in the sixties and early seventies. Authors like Amiri Imamu Baraka especially portray the black woman in minor, stereotypic roles such as the helpmate of the black man, the paragon of black motherhood, or the woman whose happiness is dependent upon her relationship with a black man.) Reasoning such as that described above only serves to prove two points: (1) that with regard to role and status, sexual politics obtains consent through the socialization of both sexes, which is to say that males are also victimized, whether or not they are aware of it; [9] (2) that identification with the oppressor is a characteristic behavior pattern of the oppressed (a theory postulated also by Frantz Fanon in Les Damnes de la Terre.)

The female black revolutionary of the 1960's was faced with deciding whether racial discrimination superseded sexual discrimination in importance. Believing their own independence was contingent upon that of the race and the improvement of life in the black community, it appears that the majority of black women submitted to male-dominated leadership.[10] Identifying their interests with those of their men, and hoping that whatever power was acquired would be shared with them, they effaced their own egos.[11] For the most part, however, their hopes were not realized.

The above-mentioned situation was in no way novel, as abolitionist-feminists were forced to make a decision under the same circumstances over a century ago. At a Convention of the American Equal Rights Association, held in New York City in 1867, Sojourner Truth, a former slave, addressed the issue of women's rights versus black rights, speaking on behalf of the doubly oppressed:

> I feel that if I have to answer for the deeds done in my body just as much as a man, I have a right to have just as much as a man. There is a great stir about colored men getting their rights, but not a word about the colored women; and if colored men get their rights, and not colored women theirs, you see the colored men will be masters over the women and

it will be just as bad as before. ... I want women to have their rights. In the courts women have no voice; nobody speaks for them. I wish woman to have her voice among the pettifoggers. If it is not a fit place for women, it is unfit for men to be there.[12]

Of course, there are many contemporary black women who have rejected the path of submission and ego obliteration. Among their numbers are various writers, who express their convictions through the medium of their art, much of which is not well received by black audiences. In the foreword of the publication, In the Memory and Spirit of Frances, Zora and Lorraine, Juliette Bowles makes the following comments:

There were the denouncements of efforts by women writers who dealt frankly with problems of black inter-personal (male/female) relations. They were called "divisive," "dyke(s)'; and pawns of a white conspiratorial mass media. Very few women authors treating themes of sexual politics in their works have gone unscathed by the fire: Ntozake Shange, Gayl Jones, Alice Walker, Toni Morrison, Barbara Smith, Michelle Wallace have all received some of this criticism. The nature and source of the castigation varies with the authors. It is black men, almost entirely, who object to "Colored Girls," while unfavorable reviews of Wallace come from black women writers and critics as well as from black men.[13]

The point was stressed earlier in this chapter that paternalism perpetuates itself through the socialization of both sexes. The following hypothesis is a possible explanation for the negative responses aroused by the authors mentioned in the above excerpt: if men are socialized to view dominance and subordination as desired masculine attributes, it is logical to assume that women are programmed to believe their status derives from that of their men. By openly rejecting such reasoning, Morrison, Walker, and others like them become targets for hostile criticism. As with most artists in America, however, they create to satisfy personal needs. They are revolutionary to the extent that they are committed to showing conditions that should be changed. To borrow an expression that was rather popular during the protest era, "they tell it like it is, not like it's supposed to be," demonstrating in singular fashion, that the individual who has no concept of his own worth is of little value to anyone else.

Every individual living within a society must, to some extent, engage in role playing, but role playing becomes hazardous when carried to such an extreme as to be confused with reality. Since racism, sexism, and paternalism compel individuals to assume preordained roles, these doctrines have a powerful, negative impact upon the maturation of the sense of identity and self-image of all involved, and they prove to be especially toxic for members of the subordinate group.

The novel Sula is a statement of protest opposing traditional American socialization, a process that achieves its ends through manipulation and alienation. A novel of extremes, Sula, like The Bluest Eye, analyzes relationships of love and hatred, perseverance and surrender, establishment and displacement, apprehension and assurance. The author uses it as a medium with which to comment upon the long established customs and norms that contribute to the estrangement of group from group, husband from wife, parent from child, and the individual from himself. The characters portrayed in this work often display remarkable courage and dogged determination in dealing with the obstacles threatening their physical survival; however, Morrison subtly suggests that self-confrontation, i.e., coming to terms with one's own perception of life and oneself, often enables the individual to better handle those problems stemming from external sources.

In early sections of her novels, Morrison is inclined to introduce images which recur throughout the works, or scenes that are portentous of events to come. For example, the image of the flying African (a myth taken from Morrison's own family folklore) pervades the Song of Solomon, appearing in the first and final sentences of the work; the jumbled wording of the introductory paragraphs of The Bluest Eye is an omen of distortion. As the action of Sula is inaugurated, the motif of the "victim" emerges as predominant and recurs throughout the novel in various forms. As opposed to The

Bluest Eye, which is narrated from the standpoint of a child, Sula deals with a more complex view of life. The major predicament the author considers is twofold in nature: (1) the effect of racism upon black identity formation; (2) the effect of racism and sexism upon the identity formation of the black female. In the first chapter of the novel, Morrison recounts the history of the "Bottom," the Negro section of Medallion, Ohio, a small town on the Ohio River. Her brief chronicle describing the origin of the Bottom and its physical setting is quite effective in creating the particular aura of resignation so characteristic of the majority of the inhabitants of that quarter. The author interjects the first image of the "powerless victim" by introducing the themes of dispossession and displacement, difficulties familiar to black Americans since the time of Reconstruction. By interposing such topics, she seeks to establish a bond of mutual suffering and understanding between characters of the novel and her audience; for although segregation and housing discrimination are now legally outlawed in America, there remains a segment(s) of society, which continues to experience repercussions related to those practices. The dispossession and displacement of families, as Morrison describes it, is a malaise that currently plagues the poverty-stricken in the nation's major, Northern urban centers. Approximately fifteen to twenty years ago, whites made a mass exodus from cities to suburbs, leaving tracks of vacant houses and ruptured municipal economies. Today the trend has been reversed, as they stream back into crowded metropolitan areas, since re-populated by immigrants from Southern rural areas. Severe housing shortages have made the redevelopment and renovation of ghetto properties quite fashionable - and practical - among "liberal homesteaders," i.e., returning whites. That practice, however, poses serious consequences for the "authentic" ghetto-dweller, who can rarely afford to purchase his home. Often, when they discover that a greater profit can be realized by selling property as opposed to renting it, landlords are wont to evacuate the premises by refusing to renew rental leases. The original tenant finds himself and his family homeless, with slight chance of obtaining suitable housing elsewhere. The result of this is the displacement and separation of families, a condition the American black knows only too well. In addition, there are other important psychological ramifications to be considered. The supposition that he will continually fall victim to chance and prey to the whims of the powerful can distort the psychological functioning of the ghetto-dweller to such a degree that he conceives his self-image in the light of failure and impotence, and may well live in a state of constant despondency.[14] Such severe stress can stimulate healthy coping mechanisms in some individuals, but it is more likely to prove injurious to the psychological make-up of the person who has experienced little positive reinforcement. Having detrimental effects on interpersonal relationships, stress situations, according to social-psychologists, contribute heavily to the percentage of crime and violence that racks the ghetto areas. Unless fads or nationwide changes in cultural trends force them to move, ghetto dwellers have little hope of leaving their environment; and if that environment contributes to psychological illness and social disease, it is small wonder that those who live within its perimeters, like the Bottom-dwellers, cast their fate to the wind. The Bottom and those who live there are symbols of people everywhere, who because of historical oppression, have come to accept as truth the notion of their own impotence and inadequacy. In every case where there has been a downtrodden class of workers at the bottom, that class has been despised by those who have benefited most from their labor. Segregation (alienation) is always detrimental to its victims; but it is especially damaging when it enjoys the sanction of the law and public opinion. Through the use of analogy, Morrison impresses her audience with the helplessness and disillusionment of victims of bigotry. She describes how the avarice of the powerful brought about both the establishment and destruction of the Bottom, with no thought having been given to the needs or desires of the people forced to live there. The author thus solicits the sympathy of the reader, but simultaneously cautions that the excessively passive will always fall victim to the aggressive.

Robert Stepto has observed that the use of extensive detail, the fixation of places in time, and the fashioning of specific geographical landscapes contribute heavily to Toni Morrison's creation of the mood and sense of community in the Bottom.[16] The community itself emerges as a powerful character, somewhat like the landscapes of Thomas Hardy, exercising a stark influence over its inhabitants, who are as isolated and limited as their environment. With few exceptions, the Bottom-dwellers are presented as prisoners held captive as much by their own lethargy and narrow-mindedness as by the confines of their surroundings. This is not to imply, however, that Morrison equates prison imagery with that of the ghetto. The individual is bound either by society's conception of him or by his own concept of himself as an individual living within society, but the person who seeks positive identity must be aware that people, through various forms of thought and behavior, may project upon him images which he considers incompatible with his own view of himself. He must also acknowledge the presence of danger in any attempt to change his attitude toward self and/or the world. In their rejection of positive self-image in favor of the "safety of the established," the people of the Bottom demonstrate that they elect to continue as victims of their own apathy as well as of the bigotry of their white neighbors. Despite the detrimental effects of isolation, there are those living within the ghetto who remain there by choice.

It is the character Shadrack who finally convinces a few of the Bottom-dwellers that confrontation is the first step toward transcendence.

In an interview conducted by Colette Dowling of the New York Times Magazine, Morrison (who left Lorain, Ohio at the age of seventeen) states that blacks, if they are to succeed in American society, must leave their native communities, and in so doing, cut themselves off from their old lives.[17] This amounts to double isolation, actually, since the doors to the white American mainstream generally remain closed to blacks. These comments explain the position of Shadrack, whose war experiences cut him off from the other residents of the Bottom, while racial differences separated him from mainstream America. Although originally from the Bottom, Shadrack is no longer "of" the neighborhood. He, therefore, functions primarily as a symbol in the novel - multifaceted instrument through which Morrison makes biting social and political comments about the Bottom-dwellers and American society in general. The author has a four-step theory about the evaluation of the literature of a culture, race, or nation, particularly an oppressed group:

> It begins with a reaction to the violence and protest, in which writers simply talk about how terrible things are. There follows a period of identification, when you're trying to get yourself together and find out who you are. Then comes a third period, in which you begin to use the myths, the magic, the symbols of the culture constructively - often with comedy, satire and parody. Finally there evolves a kind of conceptual notion of the ethnic experience.[18]

Sula obviously fits into the category of identification; therefore, the author is concerned with the general and the specific, with issues of national importance that affect blacks as Americans, and with those of local importance that pertain to them as blacks. Nineteen hundred nineteen was the year Shadrack returned to the Bottom to initiate National Suicide Day. But, it was also the year in which thousands of black veterans returned from fighting a war meant to "safeguard democracy for the world," only to find that their country denied them the benefits of the democratic process for which they had risked their lives. Black participation in World War I pointed out the ambivalence of the black man's position in American society and highlighted the schizophrenic nature of the American Dream, to which Gunnar Nyrdal referred as the "American Dilemma." Black identity and the dual heritage of the Afro-American, issues touched upon by W. E. B. DuBois in the August 1897 edition of Atlantic Monthly, re-emerged prominently. The culture in which the black man lives is American, but his status as a Black prevents his full participation in white American culture. While in America, the black man might escape his identity as an American, but he can never elude his racial identity. In responding to the draft, Afro-Americans answered the call to patriotism, but encountered racial bigotry in the armed forces. Black patriotic fervor did little to improve the racial situation in the States: Ku Klux Klan activity was revived and stepped up in 1915;

black migration to the North made whites more aware of black demands, but less willing to accede to them. In 1917, vicious race riots erupted in East St. Louis, Illinois, and racial hostility was directed toward black soldiers returning from the European front. These men, however, brought with them the knowledge of new experiences and changed attitudes.[19] Like Shadrack, "they knew the smell of death, but were not afraid of dying." (p. 12) Having risked their lives to defend the American way of life, they felt they had earned the right to share in it fully. When they attempted to exercise this right, violence erupted on a nation-wide scale. During the summer and fall of 1919 (The Red Summer), twenty-five major race riots raged across the nation, causing a marked rise in radicalism among Blacks. This radicalism was the spirit behind Marcus Garvey's call for a return to blackness, and Alain Locke's New Negro, which heralded the spiritual and cultural awakening within the black community, the Harlem Renaissance.

Rather imaginative in naming her characters, Morrison, as pointed out in Claudia Tate's review of Song of Solomon, suggests playful but subtle twists in meaning of the names of persons and places, e. g., the Bottom is situated up in the hills of Medallion, while the members of the Peace family are anything but peaceful. (Names like Cholly Breedlove are often ironically symbolic of the character traits of those who bear them.) If Shadrack of the Old Testament were a prophet of the Israelites, Morrison's Shadrack is the visionary of the Bottom - a modern, male Cassandra, as it were. There is much about Shadrack besides his name that reflects the biblical imagery the author so lavishly utilizes. Like John the Baptist, Shadrack calls for mass awareness on the part of his people. Like the Apostles, he is a fisherman as well as a fisher of men. Not confining his "ministry" to the ghetto area, he walks throughout the town preaching, much as the Shadrack of old walked through the flames - proving that no obstacle, not even racial bigotry, is insurmountable.

It is his war experience that both separates Shadrack from the Bottom and gives him the vocation of self-appointed prophet. Combat

fatigued and bereft of memory and identity, he has no alterna-
tive to coming to terms with himself in order to mold a new self-
concept:

> Twenty-two years old, weak, hot, frightened, not daring
> to acknowledge the fact that he didn't know who or what he
> was ... with no past, no language, no tribe, no source, no
> address book, no comb, no pencil, no clock, no pocket
> kandkerchief, no rug, no bed, no can opener, no faded post
> card, no soap, no key, no tobacco pouch, no soiled under-
> wear, and nothing, nothing, nothing to do. ... (p. 10)

Compelled to face the fear of the unknown, Shadrack is able to
take hold of his life by confronting the inevitability of death. He
thus learns that the individual can develop a positive self-image,
despite the ugliness and filth he may be forced to encounter:

> Like moonlight stealing under a window shade, an idea in-
> sinuated itself: his earlier desire to see his own face. He
> looked for a mirror, there was none. Finally, keeping his
> hands carefully behind his back, he made his way to the
> toilet bowl and peeped in. ... There in the toilet water, he
> saw a grave black face. A black so definite, so unequivocal,
> it astonished him. He had been harboring a skittish appre-
> hension that he was not real. ... But when the blackness
> greeted him with its indisputable presence, he wanted noth-
> ing more. (p. 11)

Having learned that fear can be controlled only if it is consciously
recognized, Shadrack institutes National Suicide Day as a means
to overcome the fear of dying by meeting, head on, the aspect of
death. James Baldwin writes, "If man is to achieve identity, he
must live with the sense of reality of both his life and death."[23]
The logic of this is lost on or unknown to most of the Bottom-
dwellers, who cling to their self-imposed limitations: "Once the
people understood the boundaries and nature of his (Shadrack's)
madness, they could fit him, so to speak, into the scheme of
things." (p. 13) Around such an atmosphere of apathy and restric-
tion is the magic of Sula woven.

In the sense that it concerns itself with the feeling and affairs of women and the roles they assume, whether by choice or force, Sula is fundamentally a woman's novel. Even though a good deal of the action of the work derives from the consequences of male/ female relationships, it is the self-perception of the woman and her subsequent reactions to self-concept that are the central issues of the novel. The male characters undergo no development, occupy no major roles (with the possible exception of Shadrack), and are important only because of the reactions they might prompt or provoke from the females.

In an intricately woven pattern of fact and folklore, Morrison makes a masterly display of knowledge gleaned from the areas of history, traditional myth and lore, and classical antiquity. Since the author taught Humanisties at various universities for almost a decade, the reader is not at all surprised to find that the central characters of Sula are, after a fashion, patterned after female prototypes, the identity of whom is subtly suggested by the names. For example, as Eve is traditionally held to be the "Urmutter" to whom both the beginning and the Fall of mankind are attributed, Eva Peace, Sula's grandmother, is also the materfamilias of her own clan. It is Eva's personal vindictiveness which does irreparable damage to her descnedants, and those who come in close contact with them, just as Mother Eve's flaw is said to have cursed the human race.

In like manner, the names of some of the male characters are subtly ironic. Sula's father, Rekus, is very possibly modeled after the Rhoecus of mythological fame, whose involvement with a wood nymph, though honorable, proved to be his undoing. Morrison's Rekus, whom the reader does not encounter personally, had to contend with a nymph of his own, in the person of his wife, Hannah. After three years of marriage to her, Rekus died. Eva's husband, Boy-Boy, is not even granted the dignity of a proper given name. That his nickname is the double reiteration of a word black males consider a term of disparagement - Boy! - might be a reflection of the low esteem with which the author seems to regard him. With this complicated intertwining of names, lives, and events, Morrison undertakes the task suggested by the title of Michelle Wallace's pub-

lication, namely the examination of the image of <u>The Black Macho</u>
<u>and the Myth of the Superwoman.</u>

Although Morrison opens her novel with the foregoing panorama,
<u>Sula</u> is the story of the friendship of Nel Wright and Sula Peace,
two black girls who seek solace in each other's company because
they share the pain of acute loneliness, and find self-fulfillment
because they share the common bond of being young, black, and
female in a world that is commonly geared to meet the designs of
mature, white males:

> Because each had discovered years before that they were
> neither white nor male, and that all freedom and triumph
> was forbidden to them, they had set about creating some-
> thing else to be. Their meeting was fortunate, for it let
> them use each other to grow on. Daughters of distant
> mothers and incomprehensible fathers (Sula's because he
> was dead; Nel's because he wasn't), they found in each
> other's eyes the intimacy they were looking for. (pp. 44-45)

From drastically different social backgrounds, Nel and Sula are
bound by factors much stronger than those which might tend to
separate them. From the perspective of this thesis, one very important common factor is that each girl comes from a household
where the dominant force is obviously a female, who maintains
her power through subordinating and manipulating others. The
black family has long been falsely viewed as being matriarchal in
form; but although the Peace and Wright households are, in essence, matrifocal, they do not comply with the theories proposed
by the <u>Moynihan Report</u> of 1965. According to Daniel Moynihan,
blacks experience a great deal of discord in their relationships
with mainstream America, because the black family structure has
deteriorated. Morrison proposes, however, that it is the pressures and false values forced upon blacks by white society that
hamper the stability of the black family. Eva Peace and Helene
Wright are both formidable women who have been permanently
scarred by emotional and psychological experiences of the past.
Consciously or unconsciously, they inflict pain on others - generally family members - in an effort to protect themselves or re-
taliate for past injuries. The reader must understand Helene and

Eva, not merely because of their familial ties with Nel and Sula, but because the two girls are really extensions of the personalities of their older relatives.

Despite dissimilar origins and life-styles, Helen and Eva have experienced similar encounters in life, each having been the victim of a patriarchal system which regarded women as chattel property. Each had come to Medallion as a young bride seeking a new life, and remained there because the town offered a retreat of sorts from realities they preferred to ignore. Both Helene and Eva are persons of consequence in the Bottom, although situated at different ends of the social ladder, and influence the lives of others through example and suggestion.

The daughter of a New Orleans Creole prostitute and an unknown father, Helene had been reared by a fanatically religious grandmother, who was obsessed, outwardly at least, with form and decorum. The grandmother passes this obsession on to Helene, warning her constantly to guard against any possible taint of profligacy inherited from her mother. Morrison employs two devices to emphasize the fanaticism of the old woman. First her name, Cecile Sabat, lends significance to her behavior. St. Cecilia, undoubtedly Mme Sabat's patron saint, was martyred because she refused to break a vow that dedicated her virginity to God. For this reason, the Roman Catholic Church honors her as the patronness of purity and virginity. Sabat is a derivative of the Hebrew word Shabbath, meaning day of religious devotion (sabbath). The author also notes that at least four statues of the Blessed Virgin grace the house of Cecile Sabat (three in the living room alone), and that Helene had grown up "under the dolesome eyes of the Virgin Mary," who, thus described, could only be the Mater Dolorosa, or Sorrowing Mother. By steering Helene into marriage with Wiley Wright, Cecile manages to settle the girl properly and comfortably in middle class life, while she herself escapes the possibility of adding new dimensions to her own position as the sorrowing mother of a "fallen" child. Ever-so-subtly, however, Morrison points out a possible side of Cecile and Helene, which having little to do with saints or holiness, has long been associated with black women. The courtship and marriage of Helene and Wiley is explained with one sentence; but within that sentence is a wealth of suggestion:

> So when Wiley Wright came to visit his Great Aunt Cecile in New Orleans, his enchantment with the pretty Helene became a marriage proposal - under the pressure of both women. (p. 15)

The reader is eventually struck by the idea that someone enchanted must be pressured into an act which should appeal to him very much, that is of course, unless the term "enchanted" is being used in its literal sense. That Helene participated in applying this pressure is not at all in keeping with her image of a sheltered, demure young innocent. Rather, her behavior calls to mind another temptress of the same name, whose beauty is said to have launched a thousand ships. Finally, the mention of numerous religious statues (charms or fetishes in some cultures) and the New Orleans setting for these scenes tend to hint at the involvement or influence of the power of voodoo. Among the most noted accomplishments of the voodoo enchanter is the ability to obtain and hold a much desired lover. Helene manages both, proving that her husband is not so clever, as his name might imply.

An architectural teratism, Number 7 Carpenter's Road is creation, possession, and dominion of Eva, a bitter authoritative woman, who attempts to direct and diagram the actions of those who live in her house in much the same manner as she designed the edifice itself. Morrison goes to great lengths to describe the strcuture, which, like its owner, is both imposing and distorted. A contributing factor to Eva's psychological disorder, but certainly not its source, is the treatment she received at the hands of her husband, Boy-Boy. After three children, five years of marriage, and handing out much abuse, Boy-Boy deserts his wife and family, leaving them no means of support or survival. At a time when employment opportunities for black women are extremely limited, Eva is forced to choose between work which will separate her from her children from five-thirty in the morning until eight at night (the eldest child is not yet five), or watching them starve before her eyes. Having to use a bit of lard, her last food staple, as a lubricant to manually relieve the locked bowels of her infant son sets her on a course of action that ultimately divests Eva of a leg, but also solves her family's financial dilemma. Even this self-inflicted physical mutilation does not impair Eva's psychological health to the same extent as her hatred of Boy-Boy, which ultimately causes her to retire from interaction with all but a few, and give her life over to manipulating and maneuvering those under her domain.

Eva's is a contradictory personality. Although a victim of masculine abuse herself, her actions show a marked preference for males, which is reflected in the treatment of her own children. "She would lie in bed with the baby boy, the two girls wrapped in quilts on the floor thinking." (p. 28) A streak of malice can be detected in her interactions with males, however, even when she performs a supposed act of charity. It appears that men afford her the opportunity for vicarious revenge against Boy-Boy for his scorn and rejection of her as a woman. Nowhere is this more obvious than in her handling of the "deweys," the three under-privileged boys for whom she provides room and board. As soon as each child comes to her, he is promptly stripped of name and identity, and renamed "Dewey." In so doing, Eva robs each of his individuality, an action characteristic of slavery, and succeeds in molding three distinct personalities into one:

> Slowly each boy came out of whatever cocoon he was in at the time his mother or somebody gave him away, and accepted Eva's view, becoming in fact as well as in name a dewey - joining with the other two to become a trinity with a plural name ... inseparable, loving no one and nothing but themselves. (p. 33)

There is also a striking dichotomy in Eva's image as a mother. On one hand, her maternal instinct is so strong, it drives her to self-mutilation to save her children from starvation, or on another occasion, to jump from the third-story window of a house to save her daughter from burning alive. She cannot, on the other hand, give normal expression to her love, which is deeply buried and tragically marred by the hatred she bears her children's father. Hers is a conditional love, passionate in rewarding or punishing, as depicted in the deliberate incineration of her drug-addicted son, Plum. Eva interpreted this action of hers not as murder, but as the second occasion on which she was forced to rescue Plum from a slow, painful, and consuming death. One wonders, however, why Eva's most profound acts of love must always extend even beyond the limits of the extreme - a characteristic of Sula's personality as well.

Just as she uses a key sentence to suggest that there is an air of the preternatural about Helene, Morrison does the same in the case of Eva, although the image created in the latter instance is that of the all-knowing conjure woman, rather than the seductive enchantress: "... and a one-legged grandmother named Eva handed you goobers from deep inside her pockets or read you a dream." (p. 25) In The Folk Beliefs of the Southern Negro, New-bell N. Pucket identifies the peanut as a plant of African origin, traditionally linked with witchcraft. By dispensing the fruits of this plant and interpreting dreams, a talent attributed to conjure doctors, Eva intimates that she, too, is linked with the supernatural.

Rejected by her thirteen-year-old mother, Helene Wright grew up knowing very little affection, and in her status as a married woman, she was regarded more as an object of adoration than a human being requiring love. Thus thwarted in her emotional development, Helene came to view middle class respectability as the virtue to compensate for other losses, and settled comfortably into the role of wife and mother. Decorum demands adherence to certain behavioral codes, which in turn call for a degree of self-denial. Payment for this sense of propriety was not so severe for Helene, however, as for her daughter, Nel, whose sense of individuality was forfeited: "Under Helene's hand, the girl became obedient and polite. Any enthusiasms that little Nel showed were calmed by the mother until she drove her daughter's imagination underground." (p. 16) With Helene's more rustic counterpart, the case was quite the opposite. A self-made woman, Eva cared little for conventional behavior and indulged her very whim, even if it were at the expense of her offspring, to whom she passed on this trait. Morrison describes the Peace children as having grown up "stealthily under Eva's distant eye, and prey to her idiosyncrasies," as opposed to Helene's rearing, which was carried out under the strict supervision of an ultra-conservative grandmother. Since there can be very little order in a household where whimsical indulgence is the rule rather than the exception, Sula's rearing was as erratic and turbid as Nel's was paced and disciplined; but instead of impairing the union of the two girls, their contrapositive upbringings only served to bring them closer together, each complementing the other. With this merger of opposites, Morrison introduces a theme later expounded more fully in the Song of Solomon, namely the plurality of aspects of the black experience in America. In its initial stages, the bond between Sula and Nel symbolizes the positive results to be gleaned once the black individual can embrace all aspects of his personality and heritage. Had it not changed from a state of reciprocal support to one of dependency, the affiliation between Sula and Nel could be regarded as psychologically healthy, rather than merely emotionally gratifying. That an alteration does occur, however, is suggested by the the events of 1922, and definitely evidenced by those of the following year.

In 1922, the girls' friendship was two years old and very intense-fortified by the onset of puberty, which broadened their interests and set them to exploring together the mysteries of life and the world of men. The author shows that Nel, whose family life is normal in the conventional sense, is seemingly the stronger of the two, while Sula is described as lacking the means for emotional sustenance. In three separate incidents, Morrison shows that Nel, in effect, becomes the stabilizing influence in Sula's life - the only person able to summon a sustained emotional response from her. The unhealthy dependence is first suggested in the confrontation between the girls and four white adolescents, where Sula, in a manner reminiscent of her grandmother, mutilates herself for the sake of a loved one. This drastic measure produces the desired effect and jolts the assailants; but it shocks Nel as well. By spilling her blood in defense of her friend, Sula symbolically seals the covenant between them. As their common bond grows progressively stronger, Nel supplants all others in Sula's affections, culminating with the replacement of Sula's mother, Hannah. This is the second indication of imbalance.

Hannah, whose name means grace and beauty, is hedonism personified. The imagery used to describe her is ironically reminiscent of that which appears in the Canticle of Canticles ("Song of Solomon"). But her flawless physical beauty is tinged by the imperfections of her character - results of her mother's influence. Although lacking Eva's guile and bitterness, Hannah is a replica of her mother, gratifying her desires without giving thought to the emotional needs of others, her daughter included. Widowed when Sula was three, Hannah moved back to her mother's house and settled into the old routine of self-indulgence, which for her was almost synonymous with sexual gratification. Like Eva, she regarded men as objects to be used. The sexual act is not an act of love, but a means of physical release: " ... Hannah was fastidious about whom she slept with. She would fuck practically anything, but sleeping with someone implied for her a measure of trust and a definite commitment. " (p. 37) Never having known paternal love, she was unaware that the relationship between male and female could be anything besides physical. Having received no affection as a child, she could give none, which meant that Sula received neither demonstrative love nor proper example. Morrison's view of the "mystical" bond between mother and child makes allowances for many flaws. The relationship between Sula and her mother is acceptable to both until this statement of Hannah's, "You love her, like I love Sula. I just don't like her (Sula). That's the difference, " gives Sula license to dissolve the bond, and channel to Nel the love previously reserved for Hannah.

The third event to permanently solder the fates of Nel and Sula is the accidental death of Chicken Little, for which Sula is responsible. Occuring on the same day that Sula hears Hannah's statement of rejection, the accident and the ramifications thereof bind the two girls even closer by making each the guardian of the conscience of the other.

Gothic in the depiction of horror and graphic in description, Hannah's death scene, set in 1923, marks the occasion of self-confrontation for Eva. The consummation of the mother (Hannah) by raging flames, passively witnessed by an interested daughter, symbolizes the extremity of the psychic disorders which can result from profuse estrangement or alientation. Paradoxically, Hannah's agonizing demise provides Sula the opportunity to demonstrate emotional severance, and Eva the occasion to display the materal love, which surges too late to be of any benefit. More importantly, the incident establishes enmity between Eva and her granddaughter, in whom she recognizes the failings of her family. Eva realizes that she is responsible for the disaster to some degree. In Sula, she comes face to face with the negative results of her efforts at manipulation. There are multiple causes for Hannah's death, most of which can be traced back to the matriarch. It is Eva who (1) fails to read the inauspicious portents that foreshadow the holocaust, (2) profanes her own body (sacrificing her leg in return for payment), and thus deprives herself of the mobility which might have enabled her to save Hannah's life, (3) must accept the ultimate responsibility for the fiery death of a second of her children, since it is the ego-centricity and self-indulgence she fostered in her offspring that enable Sula to idly look on as her mother is engulfed by the flames. In Morrison's words:

> Lying in the colored ward of the hospital... Eva mused over the perfection of the judgment against her. She remembered the wedding dream and recalled that weddings always meant death. ... She remembered something else, too, and try as she might to deny it, she knew that as she lay on the ground trying to drag herself though the sweet peas and clover to get to Hannah, she had seen Sula standing on the back porch just looking. When Eva ... mentioned what she thought she'd seen to a few friends, they said it was natural. Sula was probably struck dumb, as anybody would be who saw her own mama burn up. Eva said yes, but inside she disagreed and remained convinced that Sula had watched Hannah burn not because she was paralyzed, but because she was interested. (p. 67)

Sula reminds Eva that the guilt associated with the deaths of Hannah and Plum amounts to a personal affront to her - a suggestion that Boy-Boy had been justified in deserting a woman who was "a failure in the roles of wife and mother."

The author focuses closely upon the manner in which marriage is regarded by male and female alike. Those social values which seek to define a woman only in terms of her relationship with a man, or claim that the black woman's happiness is dependent upon a strong black man are adamantly rejected.

Regardless of social or economic standing, the residents of the Bottom all share the common belief that a woman alone is an incomplete being, who can find respectability and fulfillment only in the role of some man's mate. Tragically, the same women who are the victims of this system help to perpetuate it. Nel Wright is a classic example of such a one.

Marriage for Nel constitues embracing the very same repressive values that left her bereft of imagination and a distinct sense of self:

> Except for an occasional leadership role with Sula, she had no aggression. Her parents had succeeded in rubbing down to a dull glow any sparkle or splutter she had. ... During all of her girlhood, the only respite Nel had from her stern and undemonstrative parents was Sula. (p. 72)

Because of her upbringing, Nel does not - cannot - see anything singular about herself, i.e., she recognizes her individuality only when it is mirrored through someone other than herself. By marrying Jude Greene, she dissolves the bond of interdependence she shares with Sula, only to substitute her husband in place of her friend:

> Nel's response to Jude's shame and anger selected her away from Sula. And greater than her friendship was this new feeling of being needed by someone who saw her singly. (p. 72)

Marriage provides her the means of personal fulfillment and satisfies the expectation of the community and her mother, who saw "her only child's wedding as the culmination of all she had been, thought, or done in this world"; however, her attitude toward marriage hinders her growth, so that she, like the Deweys, remains stunted.

That the men of the Bottom view marriage as a badge is expressed in the portrayal of Jude, for whom marrying Nel is an expression of "manhood" - an act of defiance intended to flaunt his masculinity:

> So it was rage, rage and a determination to take on a man's role anyway that made him press Nel about settling down. He

needed some of his appetites filled, some posture of adult-hood recognized. ... He chose the girl who had always been kind, who had never seemed hell-bent to marry, who made the whole venture seem like his idea, his conquest. (p. 71)

Regardless of whom he might have married, Jude's wife would have been a mere commodity who added new dimension to his image and identity:

The more he thought about marriage, the more attractive it became. Whatever his fortune, whatever the cut of his gar-ment, there would always be the hem - the tuck and the fold that hid his raveling edges.... Without that someone, he was a waiter hanging around the kitchen like a woman. With her, he was head of a household, pinned to an unsatisfactory job out of necessity. The two of them together would make one Jude. (p. 71)

Rather than forge an image and a set of values meaningful to him-self, Jude conforms to the expectations of society, betraying, like Judas, himself and those who had loved and trusted him. Since the meaning of human inter-realtionships does not exceed the limits of outward display where he is concerned, it is not surprising to find that Jude's illicit love affair with Sula, ten years later, results first in the desertion of his family, and second in his leaving Me-dallion altogether, after Sula discards him. According to the men-tality of the Bottom, a man whose attention can be dismissed by a woman is really less than a man.

Sula left the Bottom as a girl, but returned a woman. An absence of ten years, the benefits of education and travel, and the exposure that results from novel experiences add new dimension to her per-sonality, so that she, like Shadrack, is no longer of the community, although the Bottom is her birthplace. In her evolved state, Sula is a living criticism of the horrific lives of resignation led by the people of the community. The ensuing encounters between them and herself serve to re-emphasize the importance Morrison attaches to the development of the complete human being, and the respect she demands for the rights of the individual.

Having run away from what she subconsciously perceived as the pain of rejection, which is what Nel's marriage really amounts to for her, Sula seeks fulfillment in other sources. The realization that completion and not companionship is what she desires brings her back to Medallion; for as she tells Nel, people are the same world over:

> Tell me about it. The big city.
> Big is all it is.   A big Medallion. (p. 85)

Sula seeks completion in novel experience, and rejection of the status quo is the most unique situation ever to exist in Medallion. Renouncing the traditional roles the women of Medallion are expected to assume, Sula vehemently denounces her grandmother, whom she eventually has committed to a sanitarium for the aged, and any of her neighbors who might be inclined to snatch away her independence:

> And I'll split this town in two and everything in it before
> I'll let you put it out! (p. 80)

Despite the enlightening results of her worldly experiences, Sula, like Nel and the other residents of the Bottom, has yet to learn a most valuable lesson, i.e., that each person has within himself the means necessary for self-fulfillment. Psychological dependence upon another prohibits the development of selfhood. Rejection by Hannah and Nel, and the death of Chicken Little damage Sula's psyche, causing her to close herself to all feelings except pure sensation. Morrison describes the adult Sula as a merger of Eva's arrogance, Hannah's self-indulgence, and a twist that was all her own imagination - but there is no mention of ego, or a conception of who or what she is. Her actions indicate that she does not view herself in terms of other's expectations. Although she might not seek identity or self-worth in the expectations or opinions of others, she does thrive on the reactions or responses her behavior can summon from them. She is, therefore, still seeking completion from without instead of within:

> She had no center, no speck around which to grow. In the
> midst of a pleasant conversation with someone, she might
> say, "Why do you chew with your mouth open?" not because

the answer interested her, but because she wanted to see the person's face change rapidly. (p. 103)

In essence, Sula, like her grandmother before her, manipulates others to avenge the injury she has been made to suffer, although her efforts appear to be made subconsciously, whereas Eva's had been deliberate. Her casual affairs cease, however, once Ajax enters her life. It is this one serious affair that proves to be Sula's undoing, for it makes her vulnerable to the effects of conventionality she had resisted so long.

In the depiction of Ajax, Morrison raises the issue of the double standard of the sexist society, which applauds the behavioral modes of one group, while condemning the next for exactly the same actions. Ajax is the male counterpart of Sula, in whom she eventually comes to see herself, and to recognize the deeds of her past. Like her, Ajax is a product of what is benign neglect. His home is also a matrifocal domicile, where the reigning monarch controls the puppet strings of her seven sons (the mystical number where sons are concerned) and definitely traffics with the spirit world - the author identifies her outright as an evil conjure woman. Although quite a ladies' man, Ajax bears genuine affection for one woman only - his mother: "This woman Ajax loved, and after her - airplanes." (p. 109) Newbell N. Pucket attributes this bond to the influence of the West African heritage of the black American: "Dominant affection in the West African home is the intense devotion of the African male to his mother."[21] Morrison, however, is of an opposing opinion, and sees the situation as having been deliberately contrived by the sorceress.

Ajax's love of airplanes is also symbolic of the kind of man he is. A symbol of flight, the airplane re-introduces the motif of transcendence, but it is a machine, an artificial means of flight utilized by those incapable of soaring by their own power. In this same way, Ajax uses women to transcend the monotony induced by his constant idleness. Frequent reference to his golden or amber-colored eyes, Morrison's badge of the heterodoxy of unorthodox characters, as compared to the description of Sula's gold-flecked eyes would indicate that Ajax is even more unconventional in his behavior than she. But all this considered, he emerges as a figure of admiration in the Bottom, while Sula is branded pariah! Insolent and conceited as Locrian Ajax of the Homeric epic, Morrison's character, A. Jacks, eventually discarded Sula in the same manner as she had discarded countless others. Since he is her male alter-ego, as stated earlier, the reader can be reasonably certain that Ajax's fate will eventually be the same as Sula's, and that of Locrian Ajax, and all of Morrison's golden-eyed characters - self-destruction.

The most prominent motifs of the final chapter of Sula, set in 1965, are those of destruction and death - the destruction of a community and a way of life, the death of a generation and an era. The author does not bemoan the fact that the old must give way to the new, for she, like the Romanticists, views death as an essential component of the cycle of life. She decries the supine, resigned attitudes of those, who in their lethargy, commit themselves and their families to existence in a death-in-life situation. From Morrison's viewpoint, the greatest tragedy of the Bottom is neither the physical collapse of the community, nor the hardships suffered by the Bottom-dwellers as a result of bigotry. Rather, she condemns the apathy that allows human beings to go zombie-like through life, without knowing who they are; what they, and not society, expect from life; and what they, as unique individuals, can contribute to it. She admonishes the reader through characters who vegetate, i.e., live a whole lifetime without seeking a positive meaning for life - characters like Eva who does not find happiness because she is obsessed with rejecting what she has been taught to perceive as the negative aspects of her personality. According to the ancient Greeks, the tragedy of death involves not the demise of the individual's body, but the sinking of his memory into oblivion. Just so, Morrison does not lament the fall of the Bottom, but the meaningless lives and empty years spent in weary anticipation of the event.

Notes

[1]Shulamith Firestone, The Dialectics of Sex: the Case for Feminist Revolution (New York: William Morrow, 1970), p.105.

[2]Kate Millett, Sexual Politics (New York: Ballantine Books, 1970), p.156.

[3]Millett, p.78.

[4]Millett, pp.78-80.

[5]Marshall H. Segall, Human Behavior and Public Policy (New York: Pergamon Press, 1976), p.159.

[6]H. Carleton Marlow and Harrison M. Davis, The American Search for Woman (Santa Barbara: Clio Books, 1976), p.232.

[7]Rosa Parks' refusal to relinquish her bus seat to a white commuter was the catalyst which started the Montgomery Alabama Bus Boycott, led by Dr. Martin Luther King, Jr.

[8]Millett, p.35.

[9]Segall, p.161.

[10]Gerda Lerner, Black Women in White America (New York: Vintage Books, 1972), p.563.

[11]Segall, p.163.

[12]Juliette Bowles, ed., In the Memory and Spirit of Frances, Zora, and Lorraine: Essays and Interviews on Black Women and Writing (Washington, D.C.: Institute for the Arts and Humanities, Howard University, 1979), p.iii.

[13]Lerner, pp.569-70.

[14]Alexander Thomas and Samuel Sillen, Racism and Psychiatry (New York: Brunner/Mazel, 1972), p.45.

[15]Andrew Billingsley, Black Families, pp.90-91.

[16]Robert B. Stepto, "Intimate Things in Place," p.213.

[17]Colette Dowling, "The Song of Toni Morrison," New York Times Magazine, 20 May 1979, p.58.

[18]Michael J. Bandler, "Novelist Toni Morrison: 'We Bear Witness,'" Africa Woman, Sept.-Oct. 1979, p.28.

[19]Norman Coombs, The Black Experience in America (New York: Twayne Publishers, 1972), p.114.

[20]James Baldwin, The Fire Next Time (New York: Dial Press, 1963), p.106.

[21]Newbell Niles Pucket, Folk Beliefs of the Southern Negro (New York: Dover Publication, 1969), pp.22-23.

Chapter 4

SONG OF SOLOMON: BLACK IDENTITY AND
THE BOURGEOISIE

American culture is predominantly middle class in ethos if not in
actual practice.[1] For this reason, it appears that much of the emotional drive of the population is aimed toward self-betterment,
which is interpreted as the ongoing acquisition and enjoyment of
material goods. Those who aspire for middle-class status struggle to eradicate or diminish the threat of privation. Those who have
already achieved that level often spend the remainder of their lives
in an effort to maintain their standing. The black American does
not differ from his countrymen in the aspiration to be classified as
middle-class, to join the "in crowd," as it were. In this sense, he
is as American as the next man; however, certain obstacles continue to hinder the efforts of blacks toward this goal and expose
the theory of the American melting pot as a myth. The term ac-
culturation does not pertain fully to the black experience in America. As emphatically stressed in the first chapter of this dissertation, white American society has generally been closed to blacks,
a condition which has limited the level of black adoption of Anglo-
European culture. Over the years, however, blacks have obstinate-
ly persisted in the desire to partake of the activities of the mainstream, though to this day that desire has not been fully realized.
Even though the theory of the melting pot is still only an idea, the
chances that it might materialize are slightly more feasible at
present than in the years prior to 1954, when the Supreme Court's
decision to condemn the policy of separate but equal in the area of
education proved to be a milestone in the struggle for black equality.
Prior to this date, segregation was the law of the land in some
places, and as such, ensured the futility of the black man's desire
for acceptance. Segregation was the catalyst that stimulated the
development and growth of a black middle class, i.e., a petit
bourgeoisie comprised of black tradesmen and professionals who
provided the black community services the white businesses could

not or would not offer. To a very great extent, the growth of the black church, black schools, and especially black banks was fostered by racism and the legal separation of the races.

In this nation, American identity is almost totally synonymous with that of the middle class; and the latter is universally associated with capitalism. The accepted goals of the middle classes are expressed chiefly in the material comforts, which are considered outward signs of success and self-esteem.[2] Because the separate but equal policy bespoke a mobility of status that existed only nominally for them, blacks strove and continue to strive for the acceptance on the part of white society by trying to equal the white man in their endeavors, including, unfortunately, mastery over men as well as things.[3] In other words, the black bourgeoisie is a very limited extension of the exploitative segment of American society. The situation existing between the strata of black society is again clearly a case of the oppressed seeking the status of oppressor. The great irony, however, lies in the fact that the ideas of the so-called "black middle class" is actually a farce. The - mental and emotional processes of a group of people who live under the same institutional and environmental conditions have a certain similarity, which is called the "basic personality."[4] In America, every black is born a member of the color caste, and as such, is subject to some form of oppression, regardless of his economic standing. To some extent, therefore, all blacks share the same basic personality. Further, as E. Franklin Frazier attests in The Black Bourgeoisie, the black middle class has no basis for influencing the American economy or the economic life of the black man, which depends upon the economy at large for its existence; hence, the black bourgeoisie is merely the more affluent segment of the divided black proletariat. The general concept of "black middle class" grew out of the efforts of one segment of the black population to pursue the American Dream, i.e., out of its desire to achieve a degree of prestige attached to relative positions in the hierarchy of status. Since they occupy the lower levels of the American social ladder, most blacks are limited to competing with each other if they are to gratify the need for social recognition. Ethnic identity varies with social class in America, and human personality varies with the conditions to which it must adapt. It stands to reason, therefore, that the same events can affect different social classes differently. As a result, there will be an emergence of variances in thought patterns and social organizations. By embracing the values of the white middle class, the black bourgeoisie runs the risk of fostering self-rejection. For example, by accepting the Anglo-European standard of physical beauty, which has historically abhorred the "Africanness" of the black American, many middle-class blacks have rejected their racial identity, and all outward manifestations thereof, in an attempt to identify with white America - hence the abundance of skin lighteners and hair straighteners on the commerical market. As expounded throughout this chapter, the denial of identity is the denial of certainty of worth; so it is possible and very probable that the psychological damage the black bourgeoisie suffers at its own hands equals that which it might cause those considered to be its subordinates:

> Lacking a cultural tradition and rejecting identification with the Negro masses on the one hand, and suffering from the contempt of the white world on the other, the black bourgeoisie has developed a deep-seated inferiority complex. In order to compensate for this feeling of inferiority, the black bourgeoisie has created in its isolation what might be described as a world of make-believe in which it attempts to escape the disdain of whites and fulfill its wish for status in American life. One of the most striking indications of the unreality of the social world which the black bourgeoisie created is its faith in the importance of Negro business enterprises owned by Negroes and catering to Negro customers.[5]

The individual laboring under illusion is enslaved, and the image of the black capitalist is certainly an illusion of one slave owning another. Self-affirmation is essentially the willingness to embrace positive and negative elements of the self in order to give new meaning to life; self-conception is involved in the individual's manner of reacting to external forces. Song of Solomon enables the reader to understand the difference between living under limitations imposed from without, and those super-imposed handicaps rising from within. In Song of Solomon, which corresponds to the

third phase of Morrison's theory of literary analysis, there is both
a presentation of effects of middle-class values on black families
and an exploration of Afro-American culture and myths that depict
the conceptual notion of the ethnic experience. The author expounds
upon the tribulations of black American life mentioned in The Bluest
Eye and Sula, and investigates another vital dimension of the black
experience, namely, the effects of white middle-class values upon
the interrelationships of blacks who adopt them. The action of the
novel takes place between 1931 and 1963. However, the work, as
Bandler says, "bridges the information gap between the black experience mirrored in legends and century-old history and the contemporary black generation that knows little about the glory amidst
the tribulations."[6]

The history of the Dead family, an American "success story" from
the perspective of the black man, stretches from the period of
Emancipation to the era of Civil Rights and militant protest. However, the political issues which emerge in Song of Solomon are
important only because of the bearing they have upon the psychological maturation of the individual characters of the novel. Racism hovers in the background, but the actual presence of white
America seldom intrudes upon the action. Most occurrences take
place within the black community, and the characters' mental development progresses as a result of their inner growth, or lack of
it.

In The Bluest Eye and Sula, the author concentrates her attention
upon explaining how or why certain events come about. But unlike
its two predecessors, Song of Solomon does not require that the
reader search his soul and ponder the events that occur. Rather,
it is intent in its pursuit of openly revealing what actually happens.
In a sense, this third novel is Morrison's own story, because so
many of its components are extracted from her family history.
Lincoln's Heaven, the farm owned by Milkman's grandfather, is
patterned after the Alabama homestead owned by the author's Indian
grandmother, the model for Hetty Byrd, who held the land by virtue
of a government grant. Morrison's family, like the Deads, lost the
land to the greed and guile of their more affluent neighbors. The

person with a sense of his own history need not conjecture about how certain events came to be if he is already aware of when and why they happened. Morrison is certainly very much attuned to who she is as an individual and from whence she stems:

> My grandfather was five years old when the Emancipation Proclamation came. He would tell later on how, when he heard people talking anxiously about it, he didn't know what they meant. In fact, he was so frightened he crawled under a bed to hide from it![7]

The custom followed by the Deads in naming their newborn children is patterned after the practice in the author's maternal family of randomly selecting a name for the infant from the Bible. The three Macon Deads not only represent different phases in the history of free blacks; but each is a facet of the personality of Morrison's father, George Wofford, a shipyard worker, who held down three jobs for seventeen years to provide for and educate his four children. Writing about forceful black men in Song of Solomon did not prove to be especially difficult or problematic for Morrison, herself a feminist, who explains it in the following manner:

> The men I have known are strong. I don't understand the notion of weak black men. I don't mean they haven't had hard lives. But my father and the other men I have known have been extraordinary. They have lived fantastic lives. They have had despair, but they also have had vigor and a sense of themselves.[8]

A quest for the vigor and sense of self whereof the author speaks is the central theme of Song of Solomon, a novel which investigates the identity crisis experienced by so many contemporary young blacks. An Erziehungsroman, the novel is the story of Macon Dead III - Milkman Dead - a young man who, towards the end of the novel, sets out to literally "find" himself. The scion of a black, petty bourgeois family, Milkman grows up with access to most of the opportunities money can provide blacks of his time. But despite the advantages of wealth, he spends the first thirty-two years of his life in a dreadful state of alienation, from which the only respite is his friendship with Guitar Baines. A vague self-concept and equally vague knowledge about his family background contribute to Milkman's perception of himself as an individual without purpose. Ignorance of his past condemns him to relive it repeatedly; for to paraphrase Hermann Kant once again, "there can be no future, i. e., progress, without knowledge of that which came before." Like young Parzival in the forest, Milkman manages to ramble through life, occasionally experiencing, but never pursuing the meaning of fleeting, intuitive sensations, which hint at distant ties of blood, e. g., his kinship with Solomon, the flying African, revealed in the second part of the novel. Milkman's rootlessness calls to mind the plight of black youth in America, who were generally confused about embracing every aspect of their identity, especially the "African Ego" about which Marion Berghan writes, until events such as the emergence of Marcus Garvey as a popular leader, the Harlem Renaissance, or the Black Power Movement of the 1960s caused periodic resurgence of black nationalism and race pride. Although he is neither happy nor satisfied with his life, lethargy leads Milkman to accept the boundaries and limitations imposed by the "significant others" in his environment, i. e., his family and peer group. Only the prospect of living the remainder of his life in the same trapped manner forces him to muster the courage needed to defy conventional authority and venture forth on his personal quest. An encounter with a figure from his father's boyhood confirms the nagging suspicion that the key to Milkman's future lies hidden, though not too deeply, in the past:

> It was a good feeling to come into a strange town and find a stranger who knew your people. All his life he'd heard the tremor in the word: "I live here, but my people..." or: "She acts like she ain't got no people," or: "Do any of your people live there?" But he hadn't known what it meant: links.[9]

The first thirty-two years of Milkman's life pass before this encounter occurs, however; and it is to those years - the protagonist's period of pre-consciousness - that the greater part of the novel is devoted.

Both Andrew Billingsley and E. Franklin Frazier comment extensively upon the emotional dilemma of the black bourgeoisie, which suffers acutely from feelings of insecurity and inferiority. To compensate for these emotional deficiencies, members of this group often engage in what Frazier calls "conspicuous consumption," i.e., frivolous spending that often exceeds their financial means. Or, they indulge in the fantasy of picturing themselves as being a part of a strong, black economic base, which sets them apart from the black masses.[10] Through the depiction of Macon Dead II, who falls into the latter category, Morrison creates a graphic sketch of the black American middle class, characterizing both positive and negative components.

The Dead family owes its middle class standing to Macon Dead II. If the reader were to categorize Song of Solomon by judging the exploits of Milkman's father, he might be tempted to classify the novel as an exemplum on the text "The love of money is the root of all evil"; for it is the desire of Macon II to grasp, own, and control all within his reach, including persons, which accounts for untold misery in the lives of those around him.[11] His obsession with money and status alienates his wife, causes his daughters to dread the sound of his voice, and even leads him to dispose of the medication that might have prolonged his father-in-law's life. The periodic recurrence of the theme of oppressed turned oppressor, or victim become victimizer in the works of Morrison impresses the reader with the seriousness the author attaches to the complex of inadequacy borne by members of the downtrodden classes. As mentioned above, the black bourgeoisie suffers doubly, since its members are alienated from their ethnic roots and frustrated by the discrimination encountered from direct contact with the whites. As Lou Benson points out, it is not hatred but lack of interest which is the opposite of positive self-evaluation, i.e., indifference is the enemy of ego. In order to counterbalance those feelings of inferiority and negate the stigma of being considered a "non-person," the victims very often become over-zealous in their support of the self-same institutions responsible for their victimization. Tragically, Macon Dead II extols the avarice and materialism which had left him and his sister, Pilate, homeless orphans years before, when wealthy white neighbors murdered their father for his land. For Macon II, this action was the first indication that the powerful view those who are economically weak as non-persons, and give no thought to their wants or needs. In capitalistic societies, the essence of power is wealth, which in turn is the equivalent of material possessions. For this reason, Macon II comes to equate materialism with security. What is perhaps more tragic, however, is the fact that in his ardent adherence to the materialistic value system, he attempts to indoctrinate his son with its principles: "Let me tell you right now the one important thing you'll ever need to know: Own things. And let the things you own own other things. Then you'll own yourself and other people too." (p. 55) Since the idea of owning things is related to the concept of self, it is relatively simple to understand how the belief that money and property attach value to the individual, drives Macon II to the point of suffering from pathological possessiveness.[12] This tendency toward acquisition is evidenced as early as his sixteenth year, when the greed for gold curdles his love for Pilate, whom he had tended since infancy. That same possessiveness colors and mars all of his personal relationships, especially that with his wife, Ruth.

The relationship between Macon II and Ruth lends added dimension to the story by considering the perspective from which the average black views the black bourgeoisie, and that from which the black middle class views itself. The hierarchy which exists within the privileged class and the code by which the membership abides are also examined. Frazier's study reveals that the original black bourgeoisie was comprised of free blacks of mixed heritage.

Miscegenation contributed to the formation of a superior class among blacks in a number of ways.[13] In a society where "white meant right and might," fair skin denoted white ancestry, and therefore was a step above skin of darker hue. White slave masters often freed and educated their offspring by black concubines, and thus contributed to the formation of a class of cultured free blacks. Even those fair-skinned blacks who were slaves, however, were usually house servants, who, because of a closer association with whites, spoke differently and affected different manners than the field servants. Following the close of Reconstruction, the nature of the black man's social world, which emerged as a result of racial segregation, was such that it resembled a small-scale replica

70

of American society, with the exception that all the members were of the black race. Ruth Foster Dead had a place among the Brahmin caste of this society by right of birth. Since the conditions of birth did not guarantee Macon II's automatic entry into the ranks of the elite, he had to satisfy other criteria to gain admittance. It was his belief that the acquisition of money and property, coupled by his marriage to Ruth, the "only child of the biggest Negro in this city" would suffice to qualify his entry. He realized too late, however, that according to the standards of the black middle class, he would always be an interloper among those whose acceptance he sought so desperately. Macon is further handicapped, because the values and standards by which the black bourgeoisie judges him are the very standards he has adopted for himself. Therefore, rejection by the black bourgeoisie is tantamount, in Macon's case, to self-rejection. He cannot see the role he plays in attacking his own sense of worth, and shifts the blame to others, particularly his wife and her father. In an attempt to compensate for the "short-comings" of his birth and background, he becomes even more avaricious and materialistic:

> Where I'd come from, the farm we had, that was nothing to them. And what I was trying to do - they didn't have any interest in that. Buying shacks in shack town, they called it. 'How's shacktown?' That's the way he'd greet me in the evening. (p. 72)

Macon considers Ruth's devotion to her father, who is his physical and cultural opposite, as rejection of himself, in much the same ways as Pecola Breedlove views Shirley Temple's beauty as a declaration of her own ugliness. Unlike Pecola, however, Macon is a fighter who does not readily acquiesce to snobbery, real or imagined! To assuage his wounded pride and maintain some sense of selfworth, he convinces himself that he never cared for his wife at all:

> I married your mother in 1917. She was sixteen, living alone with her father. I can't tell you I was in love with her. People didn't require that as much as they do now. Folks were expected to be civilized to one another, honest, and - and clear. You relied on people being what they said they were, because

there was no other way to survive. The important thing when you took a wife was that the two of you agreed on what was important. (pp. 70-71)

When self-deception fails, he resorts to physical violence to bolster his ego (e.g., he savagely strikes Ruth at the dinner table), until forcibly restrained by his son. In the article, "The Black Black Woman and the Black Middle Class," Trellie Jeffers observes that blacks have not made a violent shift from the neo-conservatism of the black middle class and its value system," for we, like them, have not shaped a direction for ourselves." Rather, many blacks cling to the all-American policy of rugged individualism at the price of personal and group destruction.[14] This observation is certainly applicable to the situation of Macon Dead II, who evolves as a psychological mutant of the boy he had been prior to the murder of his father. Morrison explains his condition in the following passage:

An old man now, who acquired things and used people to acquire more things. As the son of Macon Dead the first, he paid homage to his own father's life and death by loving what his father had loved: property, good solid property, the bountifulness of life. (But) he loved these things to excess. Owning, building, acquiring – that was his life, his future, his present, and all the history he knew. That he distorted life, bent it, for the sake of gain, was a measure of his loss at his father's death. (p. 304)

Macon II distorted life, because he himself had suffered psychological and emotional distortion. So extensive was the damage done him, that he who had seen men slay his own father for the love of money was himself driven by that same greed to slay at least one other, the old man in the forest, and possibly a second, Ruth's father. He who had been driven from his home as an orphaned child, assumed the role of slum landlord, and in turn, drove other parentless children from their homes. He who had known the insecurity and degradation of dire poverty strove to recover his dignity by forcing other unfortunates to experience the same humiliation. Such behavior explains why Morrison puts the following sentence into the mouth of one of Macon's evicted tenants: "A nigger in busi-

ness is a terrible thing to see. A terrible, terrible thing to see."
(p. 22)

Of the three Morrison novels, only Song of Solomon has a male
protagonist, and it alone is written from a supposedly male van-
tage point. Nevertheless, sexual exploitation of the female emerges as an issue of prominence in this work, just as in The Bluest
Eye and Sula, with the exception that more attention is focused on
the middle-class black woman in the most recent novel. Since the
atmosphere of this work is markedly paternalistic and materialistic, the reader expects the false sense of superiority which the
male characters assume in their dealings with the females. The
only apparent difference between the third novel and its two predecessors is the lesser degree of physical abuse directed toward
the black woman of the middle classes. In either social stratum,
however, the male is wont to vent his frustration on the female.

Milkman Dead is a true product of his environment insofar as his
relationships with women are concerned. Morrison feels, however,
that his behavior should not evoke any surprise from the audience,
since he is one of those individuals without any sense of personal
dignity. One who is unaware of his own value as an individual can
hardly be expected to be solicitous of the self-esteem of others.
The females in Milkman's life, with the exception of Pilate (and at
a later point in the novel, Circe), are rather complacent in their
acceptance of disdainful treatment, because they are victims of the
same system of socialization as he. They, however, are the subjugated and he, as the "inherently superior male," is the subjuga-
tor. Pilate, on the other hand, is the first woman to command
Milkman's grudging respect, just as a man would demand it: "And
while she looked as poor as everyone said she was, something
was missing from her eyes that should have confirmed it. (p. 37)
She was the first woman to whom he had to look up, in even the
literal respect: "And when she stood up, he all but gasped. She
was as tall as his father, head and shoulders taller than himself."
(p. 38) Most umportantly, however, she was the first person, male
or female, to arouse in him a sense of pride in himself and his
family:

> Even while he was screaming he wondered why he was sud-
> denly so defensive.... Now he was behaving with this
> strange woman as though having the name was a matter of
> deep personal pride, as though she had tried to expel him
> from a very special group, in which he not only belonged,
> but had exclusive rights. (p. 38)

Pilate, as stated above, is the exception rather than the rule.
Milkman relates condescendingly to other women, making no exceptions for mother, sisters, or lovers. All exist for the purpose
of satisfying his needs of the moment. The depiction of those relationships amounts to an illustration of the effects of middle-class
values upon the psyche-maturation and self-concept of black women
from all strata of society.

Inclinations toward accommodation and resistance dot the course of
black history in America; however, all blacks - resisters and ac-
commodationists alike - are subject to the limitations imposed by
the color caste. Sexism, as we have seen, is akin to racism in
many respects but especially in that it is as much a scourge to those
who submit to it as to those who withstand it. In America, racism
is itself a kind of classism, which is to say that the fate of the
black woman in this country is determined, to a large extent, by
racist and sexist policies, regardless of the social caste from with
the individual may stem. Forms of privation vary from one level
of society to the next, but women in all strata share in common
the humiliation of being handled as commodites instead of being
treated as human beings. The Bluest Eye and Sula focus primarily
upon the lot of the lower-class black woman, while Song of Solomon
concerns itself with the woman of the middle classes (Ruth and her
daughters), as well as her less fortunate sisters. There are ac-
commodationists and resisters among both the higher and lower
classes of black women. However, because the bourgeoisie sets
such an outstandingly high value upon propriety, the middle-class
woman, who since childhood has been indoctrinated with standards
of what is or is not socially acceptable, may be less likely to vocal-
ly or militantly oppose the status quo. Regardless of the social rank
of those considered in Morrison's novels, one message is firmly
reiterated: the person who passively submits to attacks upon his/

her psyche actually reinforces and condones the behavioral tendencies from which the assault results in the first place; one whose
individuality enables him to resist attempts at ego-obliteration
may be persecuted, but can never be humiliated by behavior stemming from the psychological deficiencies of another.

That Milkman Dead suffers so acutely from anomie is the strongest
indication that his formative years were passed under psychologically pathological conditions. It is a clue that the significant others
in his environment suffer from either the same ailment or from
some related malady. As the story unfolds, it becomes obvious
that the twelve-room house which is home to the Dead family is
equipped with every feasible implement necessary for comfortable
living except demonstrative affection and love. Described as "more
prison than palace," the edifice is merely a showcase meant to
distinguish its inhabitants from the plebians among whom they
dwell. Over the years, the children born into that home have come
to be recognized as showpieces to be displayed in the same manner
as the house itself. Ruth Foster, and later her children, were primarily symbols of their fathers' propriety and bienseance, and
secondly, the physical manifestations of the love, now remote,
their parents must have once borne each other. Ruth's rearing was
such that she saw herself as a fairytale princess, who had grown
up confident of the affection ot the reigning monarch, her father,
when in fact, she was an insignificant satellite revolving around
him, reflecting the light he cast off, thinking the same thoughts as
he, and seeing the world with the same eyes. By her own admission,
Ruth Foster Dead is a small woman, conditioned to accept and believe in her own inadequacy, so that she is incapable of independent
self-fulfillment:

> ...I was pressed small. I lived in a great big house that
> pressed me into a small package. I had no friends, only
> school mates who wanted to touch my dresses and white silk
> stockings. But I didn't think I'd ever need a friend because I
> had him.... The only person who ever really cared whether
> I lived or died ... there was, and is, no one else in the world
> who ever did. And for that, I would do anything.... I am not
> a strange woman. I am a small one. (pp. 123-124)

The image Ruth presents is treated by the author as grounds for rebuke and admonition rather than celebration. In Ruth's physical description alone - fair skin, light colored eyes, straight hair - the reader comes to recognize the clues which indicate that Morrison will treat this character with both compassion and contempt, a fact for which Leatha Simmons Mitchell scathingly takes the author to task:

> There are two kinds of women who people Morrison's tales and usually they are two different shades of black, and belong to two different castes. There are the dark-skinned (black, "heavy-brown") women who define their own existence, even if in destructive or negative terms, and there are the light-skinned (lemony), insipid, puerile, neurotic women who indulge their fantasies, earn the disgust of their husbands and have their existences defined by others. Whether they create and define themselves like Pilate and Sula, or are passive-aggressive manipulators of their husbands like Nel and Ruth, or live lives of frigid, sheltered stupor (Lena and Corinthians), the consequences of all their actions are either tragic or pathetic. Their ultimate fate is defilement, abandonment, degradation, humiliation, and violent or agonizing death. To find my sisters so encomposed and circumscribed by color distressed me greatly - almost irrationally so.[15]

The lemon-yellow complexion on which the black bourgeoisie looks as a badge of distinction is deemed by Morrison as a mark of oppression, because the character bearing this distinguishing feature must live bound by a certain code if she is to receive the adulation to which her "badge" entitles her. Because their physical and emotional resemblance to their mother bespeaks their relationship with Dr. Foster, Macon looks upon his daughters with the pride of possession and personal scorn, establishing the precedent which Milkman follows later. In Lena's own words:

> First he displayed us, then he splayed us. All our lives were like that: he would parade us like virgins through Babylon, then humiliate us like whores in Babylon. (p. 218)

Their social failure, the hesitancy or refusal to assert themselves in defense of their rights at home ensure Lena and Corinthians their father's monetary support, but also his open disgust and disdain. They are symbols of all he has struggled to achieve. However, they in no way reflect the spirit and determination which has been the driving force in his life, the only emotion he understands, the desire to acquire, own, and manipulate. In the final analysis, the only factor which saves Milkman from the fate of his sisters is the fact that he is a male and as such, enjoys more freedom and greater mobility than they. According to an unwritten code, they are expected to be subordinate to him, despite the fact that he is a number of years their junior:

> Who are you to approve or disapprove anybody or anything? I was breathing air in the world thirteen years before your lungs were even formed. Corinthians twelve.... Where do you get the right to decide our lives.... I'll tell you where. From that hog's gut that hangs down between your legs. I don't know where you will get it or who will give it to you, but mark my words, you will need more than that. (pp. 216-17)

This stinging accusation of Lena's is a denunciation of the practise of judging the action of males and females by double standards. Her words indirectly challenge Milkman to pick up the gauntlet life tosses down, and meet the challenge of living as a man, not in the fulfillment of the "macho" image, but as a developing human being, who by coincidence, is male in gender.

The most fascinating and complex of Morrison's messianic, ethereal character, Pilate Dead, of all those who fit the stereotypic description "otherworldly," is, paradoxically, the one most readily and easily understood. Although only moderately literate, Pilate is by no means an unlearned woman. The knowledge she acquires, which is symbolized by the contents of her single earring, she gleans from the experiences of life. In no way hampered by the encumberances of middle class conventionality, Pilate's lifestyle is despised by her brother, from whom she remained isolated for a number of years. When he is informed of why and how she finally sought Macon out, the reader is able to detect the hand of fate at work, for it was Pilate who bore the lion's share of the responsibility for Milkman's conception and birth. At a very early point in the novel, it becomes evident that Pilate is a link between the natural and the supernatural, and that her simplicity and innocence make her equally comfortable in either sphere. For example, her acceptance of death as part of the cycle of life releases Pilate from any inhibitions related thereto: ... one conviction crowned her efforts: since death held no terrors for her (she spoke often to the dead), she knew there was nothing to fear. (p. 149) There are, in fact, a number of things about Pilate which are reminiscent of the Greek god, Hermes, the Olympian messenger responsible for conducting the souls of the dead to Hades, but in the case of her nephew, she leads the dead to the world of the living. As a seer, Pilate is also a mouthpiece for the spirit world. When the reader encounters her for the first time, she both predicts the early birth of Milkman and lifts her voice in song as an escort for Mr. Smith, the deranged insurance man, who leaps to his death from the roof of Mercy Hospital. At the close of the novel, Pilate passes on this duty to Milkman, who sings her death-song. Whereas Hermes is the patron deity of travelers, Pilate devotes over twenty years of her life to wandering from place to place. As Hermes released his fellow god, Ares, from a wretched, long-term confinement, so too does Pilate release her sister-in-law, Ruth, from an unbearable state of compulsory celibacy and loneliness. There is also evidence that Morrison draws upon the image of the Earth Mother as a model for Pilate, who is an infinite source of nourishment for her family, just as the earth is the never-failing source of sustenance for her children. Through the portrayal of Pilate, the author offers possible answers to many of the questions posed by black youth in the 1960's and early 1970's - questions such as: what is the significance of the "real" name as opposed to the "slave" name of the American black? Or, does acceptance of his African heritage automatically cancel the American heritage of the Afro-American? Pilate's very being is an inspirational answer to the Afro-American identity seeker, as she herself is actually a fusion of the races and cultures which have contributed heavily to the makeup of the so-called "American personality." In other words, Pilate is proof that the melting pot for which America is supposedly renowned does exist in at least one sense. She is especially significant for the Afro-American, because she represents what Trellie Jeffers terms "the womb source" of black America's genetic and cultural heritage, and encompasses all the components which contribute to the whole. The black American, the author acknowledges, is a hybrid, a genetic and cultural synthesis of many factors, whose mental health depends upon his acceptance of everything of which his personality is comprised. Although the historical trend has been for blacks to reject the African Ego, Morrison would have the readers remember that the non-African elements of the black American heritage are important in their own right. Afro-American ethnicity is not African in origin, but the result of the African's experience in the new world. In creating the mood and setting for Song of Solomon, the author borrows from the African, Amerindian, and European backgrounds. For example, Geoffrey Parrinder writes that ancestor worship, communication with the dead, strong attachment to the land and fetishism are all integral elements of traditional African religions. Pilate, who is described as a natural healer, has a supportive, posthumous relationship with her father, with whom she actually converses. Though she is unaware of it, she carries his bones with her under the guise of her "inheritance." Song of Solomon abounds with folklore, most of which, according to folkloric authority, Richard M. Dorson, can be traced back to European sources.[16] For example, the belief that a physical peculiarity marks the conjurer as different from other people explains the uproar caused by Pilate's lack of a navel. Finally, the appearance of the Byrd family represents the American Indian element of the Afro-American heritage. With all this, Morrison reminds the reader that no culture is inherently inferior or superior to another, and that good and evil are not restricted to any particular race or group. Charity is charity, and depravity depravity, regardless of its source or origin.

In her extreme isolation, compassion, and concern for and about human relationships, Pilate is well able to commiserate with the wretched of the earth. By assisting in bringing about Milkman's conception and protecting the unborn child until its birth, Pilate takes on the responsibility for a life. Remembering her father's statement, "You just can't fly on off and leave a body," she realizes that her father refers to the responsibility man has to the

living as well as the dead. (p. 148) Because she helped bring him
into the world, it was Pilate's duty to prepare Milkman to face the
difficulties of living. She could not, therefore, "fly away," deserting him in the same way her grandfather, Solomon the Flying
African, had deserted his son, Jake (Pilate's father), so many
years before. In part one of the novel, Pilate is not only Milkman's
aunt, but his friend, mentor, and living link to his past. Although
she appears only briefly in part two, it is very clear that the presence of her being and all she has represented for Milkman over
the years sustain him through the ordeals of discovering who he is.
Eventually Milkman bears witness to the truth of Pilate's statement that only ignorance about himself can prevent the individual
from transcending any problem life sends his way.

Perhaps it is no coincidence that the females who figure most
prominently in Milkman's life, whether they are the "lemony yellow" women of the middle classes, or the "heavy brown" women
from the less affluent segments of black society, are all related to
him by ties of blood. These ties of kinship have a multiple purpose
in that they represent the individual components which comprise the
total black American experience; they depict the diverse personality
traits which contribute to the composition of the complete character
of Milkman Dead; they demonstrate the effects of capitalistic materialism on family and personal life.

The breakdown of traditional family ties and the repercussions of
the deliberate attempts of Macon Dead II at denying the bond of
kinship between his sister and himself are manifested in the unorthodox, and by occidental standards, incestuous relationship between his son, Milkman, and his niece, Hagar. By isolating himself and his insular family from the extended branch comprised of
Pilate, her daughter Reba, and Reba's daughter, Hagar, Macon II
seeks to cancel any connection between the two groups. Pilate is
the living link between himself and the past he elects to forget. The
forced separation only succeeds in strengthening the distorted attraction between Hagar and Milkman, because that which is forbid-
den has the tendency of appearing more exotic and enticing. Besides
giving him a tie to the past, Milkman's relationship with his aunt
and cousins provides him a means for self-expression, which in-

cludes twelve years of sexual encounters with Hagar. On the first day of their acquaintance, Hagar and Milkman are cautioned by Pilate concerning the bond of kinship between them:

> "Hagar." Pilate looked around the room. "This here is your brother, Milkman." "That ain't her brother, Mama. They cousins," the older woman (Reba) spoke. "Same thing.... I mean, what's the difference in the way you act toward, 'em? Don't you have to act the same way to both?" (p. 44)

Her admonition goes unheeded and dire consequences arise. However, Morrison, through Pilate, communicates that she is not overly concerned with the lack of conventionality of the love affair between Milkman and Hagar. The primary issue is not the profanation of a long-standing, sacred taboo, but the violation of the human dignity of an individual. What is even more horrendous for the author is the fact that Hagar herself actively contributes to that violation by defacing her own personality. When Pilate addresses Milkman and Hagar about the bond of kinship which binds them, she speaks not in the vein of the Spiessbuerger - the narrow-minded moralizer - but as a woman of wisdom, who having played a major role in ushering both her granddaughter and nephew into the world, recognizes the psychologically destructive tendencies they share in common. It appears that heredity and environment contribute much toward making Hagar even more anomic than Milkman! She finds the task of forging a future more complicated than he for various reasons: (1) she knows even less about her past than Milkman knows about his - not even her father's name; (2) the fact that she is female hinders her chances for self-determination; (3) her lower-class status does not prevent her from acquiring the values of the bourgeoisie, so that she, like her uncle Macon, craves a place among those who despise everything about her, because she represents the vestiges of their own past that they strive to forget. Since she does not have the advantages that wealth and gender make accessible to Milkman, she necessarily finds life somewhat more trying than he. However, by attaching herself to him, she experiences his world vicariously. The relationship becomes problematic when the attachment is carried to the point of becoming emotional enslavement. By making Milkman her master, Hagar puts herself in a position to be driven off once she becomes an encumbrance.

When ultimately he does reject her, as Abraham rejected another slave with the same name, she explains to Pilate that she believes the rejection came about because she is the physical antithesis of the middle-class, Anglo-European standard of beauty: "He loves silky hair ... Penny-colored hair ... And lemon-colored skin ... And gray-blue eyes ... And thin nose. He's never going to like my hair." (pp. 319-320)

She ignores the counsel given by her Milkman's friend, Guitar Baines, to find personal worth within herself: "You think because he doesn't want you anymore that he is right - that his judgment and opinion of you are correct. If he throws you out, then you are garbage.... Could you really love somebody who was aboslutely nobody without you?" (pp. 309-310) Nor does she heed Pilate, who attempts to make her see that if Milkman uses her physical appearance as criteria for rejecting her, he is essentially rejecting himself, and is not worth the effort it takes to hold him: "How can he not love your hair? It's the same hair that grows out of his armpits. The same hair that crawls up out of his crotch on up his stomach. All over his chest. The very same.... It's his hair too. He got to love it." (p. 319) In a final attempt to become the person she believes Milkman wants her to be, Hagar goes on a wild shopping spree, frantically clutching the clothes and cosmetics she sees as a symbol of middle-class values. While shopping, she is drenched in a storm, catches a chill that eventually develops into pneumonia, and dies. Ironically, as Hagar grasps the clothes, the symbols of middle-class status, in a forest hundreds of miles away, Milkman is discarding his own clothes, and experiences inner freedom for the first time in his life.

Because she does not heed the wisdom of her counselors, and because she commits spiritual suicide by enslaving herself to another individual, Hagar condemns herself to death. For Morrison has no other choice except to eliminate her, if she is to function effectively in her role as a revolutionary artist. The image that Hagar presents cannot be celebrated, though it must be acknowledged; therefore, she, like Pecola Breedlove, undergoes a ritualistic death, which both halts the spread of the contagion she carries, and admonishes the audience to find fulfillment in self. Morrison acknowledges the tragedy of Hagar's situation, but she insists firmly that the individual must accept the responsibility for his own life and death. This sentiment is voiced by Pilate for the benefit of Hagar and Ruth, the two women whose love for Milkman exceeds their self-love: "People die when they want to and if they want to. Don't nobody have to die if they don't want to." (p. 141) The wise individual guards his innermost being from all external threats. If he or she chooses to lower his/her defense, then he/she must suffer the consequence of this conscious decision, whatever it might be.

The Southern black cultural experience is an integral part of the identity-history of the Afro-American, because Afro-American history itself began in the South. Therefore, establishing a sense of identity proves to be somewhat problematic for Milkman Dead, a black man who is at least two generations removed from the Southern experience. In addition, the peculiar circumstances of his family life amount to a deliberate attempt on the part of his father to wipe out any connections with the Dead family's Southern heritage. The author makes Milkman and the audience aware of the bond between Northern and Southern blacks through the medium of Guitar Baines, Milkman's only intimate friend, who has two other important functions in the novel: (1) Guitar generally voices the sentiments the author would attribute to the black from the lower classes - it is Guitar, in fact, who first makes Milkman aware that he can move freely in and out of the different strata of black society; (2) Guitar and the Seven Days eventually come to represent the radically violent element of the Black Revolution, which emerged most forcefully after non-violent means failed to procure justice and civil rights for blacks in America. If competitive possessiveness, i. e. , the desire for the continuous, limitless gain of material goods at an ever-increasing rate, often results in a condition of pathological possessiveness for those who succeed in acquiring, it has an equally destructive impact upon those who either fail in their attempts at acquisition, or who simply have no possessions, because that lack frustrates a natural need.[17] Status seeking is an extension of the human need for respect and the desire to be admired. In capitalistic societies, where status is equated with material possessions, there is a great likelihood that the poor suffer from an exaggerated sense of inferiority and ego-deflation, which leaves an indelible scar upon the psyche. Even future monetary success cannot completely eradicate all vestiges of the psychoses that can result from such devastating experiences, as can be observed in the case of Macon Dead II. If the deprived are emotionally geared toward the principles of materialism, and do not achieve significant material success, as often happens in capitalistic societies, they can become subject to severe psychological perversions, which is precisely what Morrison depicts in the characterization of Guitar Baines.

Despite the obvious differences stemming from the disparity in their ages and social status, the bond of friendship Milkman shares with Guitar is every bit as intense as that which binds Sula Peace and Nel Wright. Although their relationship does not extend to the point of total interdependence, Guitar and Milkman do satisfy basic needs in each other. Twelve-year-old Milkman supplies Guitar with the hero-worship and ego-boosting admiration he so desperately craves to maintain his self-respect and sense of importance. The older boy provides his companion an outlet for intimate exchange and self-expression, which he does not receive at home. Boys grow into men, however, and discover that friendship requires mutual understanding, acceptance and tolerance, in addition to boyish admiration, if it is to sustain itself. To paraphrase Macon Dead II, being a whole man requires dealing with the whole truth. In the course of the last year of their friendship, it becomes quite clear that neither Guitar nor Milkman has ever honestly or openly looked within himself to discover his own "personal truth." Consequently, neither is capable of really knowing or understanding the other. Each suffers from a form of psychosis - Milkman from chronic anomie, which leaves him listless and uncaring, and Guitar from acute paranoia, which advances to schizophrenia - and each upholds the other in projecting the guilt for personal inadequacy upon the external world. In the early years of their acquaintance, their mutual support is an adequate shield against the realities of life, but because he does not have the financial assets available to his friend, Guitar is forced to function in the adult world sooner and more seriously than Milkman. Adulthood carries certain responsibilities which require the mature individual to take stock of his life and personal value system. Although he is not a member of the black bourgeoisie, Guitar, like Macon II and Hagar, has unconsciously internalized the values which actually teach him to despise himself. When judging himself by the standards of the blacks bourgeoisie, he is confronted by the image of a failure - an inferior person. Instead of repudiating the false image based upon psychotic hallucination and lies, he accepts it. Instead of establishing personal standards, he projects the "blame" for his shortcomings on the others, whom he both envies and hates. Social psychologists claim that projection is the principal defense mechanism of the acutely paranoid. As his illness progresses, Guitar loses his grip on reality, and in the manner of Macon Dead II, allows avarice to turn him savagely against one he had formerly loved.

Through the characterization of Guitar Baines, the author stresses the importance of distinguishing that which is genuinely revolutionary from the reactionary. Guitar is perfectly capable of and willing to kill for the revolution, but he neither understands, nor even recognizes the true nature of the cause he claims to espouse. In effect, he is the classic example of the rebel without a cause. Morrison does not refute the validity of Guitar's charge that a racist political system actually encourages and fosters the social ills which rack American society.

She supports his accusation with a scene set in 1955, where Guitar and other black men discuss the murder of a black youth in Mississippi. The comments of those gathered in Tommy's Barbershop to discuss the homicide represent the attitudinal changes that had taken place among blacks from the time of the first World War to the advent of the Civil Rights Movement. Reflected were general disillusionment because America had reneged on practically every promise made to blacks since the Emancipation; frustration because patriotism and heroic participation on the part of blacks in two World Wars and the Korean Conflict had not procured black civil rights in America; and angry determination to win a share in the American Dream for the black population at all cost. In 1955,

the year of the Montgomery, Alabama Bus Boycott, blacks still recalled that during World War II, German prisoners-of-war enjoyed
privileges in America that they themselves were denied; they recalled fighting on the European and Pacific fronts, while at home,
fellow blacks were denied positions in the defense industries until
1941, when A. Philip Randolph threatened to lead a black march
on Washington. (In 1948, Randolph began advocating civil disobe-
dience and mass resistance in a more desperate effort to effect
change.) In the course of Afro-American history, three methods
have been employed to bring about social change: (1) appeal to
American idealism; (2) mobilization of economic and political
strength; (3) physical force. Racism has been so deeply internalized into the white mentality that, at times, devastating means
are employed to make significant changes in the status quo. After
the first two methods failed repeatedly, blacks resorted to violence, as they felt they could no longer wait for white America to
accede to black demands, or give genuine sanction to the Civil
Rights Law enacted in 1957. In that same year, Robert F. Williams,
then head of the Monroe, North Carolina branch of the N.A.A.C.P.,
began advocating the use of violence in self-defense. In his book,
Negroes With Guns, Williams states that a racist social system
exists in the United States, because the violence at the heart of that
system goes unchallenged. The Civil Rights Movement moved gradually from the point of passive appeal to active resistance and then,
beyond the point of nonviolence. The Song of Solomon closes in 1963,
eight years after the murder of Emmett Till (the youth discussed in
the barbershop) for allegedly whistling at a white woman - the same
year in which Dr. Martin Luther King carried out A. Philip Randolph's threat to lead a peaceful march on Washington. By then,
however, there were many others who strongly advocated the use
of violence as a means of obtaining black rights, in opposition to
King's doctrine of non-violence. As a member of the black vigilante
group, the Seven Days, Guitar Bains is foremost among those who
seek an eye for an eye, and return hatred for hatred.

The author neither condemns nor condones the move toward violent
encounter, as she seems to consider that a matter for the individual
conscience to decide. It is Guitar's method of reasoning which pre-

sents such a perturbing problem for her, because he reasons thus: I am the victim of deprivation and depravity, and am therefore justified in behaving in an equally depraved manner as those who persecute me. Such "logic" is abhorrent to Morrison. In at least three separate interviews, the author has reiterated that "centuries of beastial treatment have not resulted in changing blacks into a race of beasts." As a revolutionary artist, she poses the question: of what intrinsic value to the revolution is the individual who does not value his human dignity? The year 1963 marked the close of a period of pre-consciousness for Milkman Dead and a large percentage of the black American youth of whom he is a symbol. No longer able to ignore or camouflage the harsh realities of the black condition in America, Milkman and a multitude of individuals of Afro-American extraction are compelled to make cognizant choices with regard to the standards and images which will affect their futures. Milkman must choose between seeking and establishing his identity as an independent individual or resigning himself to the prospect of foregoing his position as a unique personality and settling down in life as a symbol of Macon's wealth, Ruth's martyrdom, and Hagar's love.

Black America is faced with the choice of continuing to live in the shadow of the mainstream of white society or making a desperate bid for full citizenship. In either case, the "underdog," as it were, chooses to foresake the security of the established, challenge the status quo, and set out to forge its own destiny. Since the foundation of the future rests firmly upon the past, it is necessary that a figurative journey into bygone times be undertaken, in order to trace the roots of Milkman and Afro-America in general. A modern-day Jedermann, Milkman receives the summons of life, and in answering it, leaves behind Fellowship, Cousin, and Kindred, although he does take a few of the Goods binding him to the old life (which he very shortly loses). Like the protagonist of the morality play, he sets out on the Joycean journey, relying heavily upon Beauty, Strength, Discretion, and the Five Wits, but ultimately comes to the realization that self-confrontation, as he has begun to experience it, truth, and the security afforded by Pilate's love have more than adequately prepared him to see the journey through to its end.

It is Pilate who gives Milkman the means to life, pride, and identity. However, while the novel is situated in the Northern setting, even Pilate's influence has very little corrective effect upon her nephew, whose life-style causes him to bear a strong resemblance to the peacock that periodically appears throughout the work. Both Milkman and the peacock endure the frustration of not being able to satisfy a natural impulse; however, the bird is hindered by natural causes. Because it is a bird, the impulse to fly is ingrained in the peacock's very nature. A direct descendant of the Flying African, Milkman, too, has inherited the inclination toward flight; and yet, like the peacock which is weighted down by its magnificent plumage, he is thwarted in his desire by the exterior trappings of wealth, status, and middle class propriety.

His sojourn in the South marks a turning point for Milkman as an individual as well as in his capacity of symbol of black American youth, because that period marks the first time in his life that Milkman must do himself that which he has always requested of others: namely, he is forced to discard the exterior facade of his life, consider the man he is from within, and bear the responsibility of his own life. The Southern journey is patterned after the Romantic standard which rejects the corruption of the urban setting and favours the purity and perfection of the natural, rural setting that puts men on equal footing with each other and the other creatures of nature. Morrison very aptly demonstrates this in the depicition of the hunt, where Milkman stalks a cougar, and is tracked in turn by Guitar.

Shedding the exterior symbols of status is an act of ritualistic purification, since for the first time in his life, Milkman is forced to relate to others (and to himself) simply as "himself." Morrison writes:

> Under the moon, on the ground, alone ... the cacoon that
> was 'personality' gave way.... He was only his breath,
> coming slower now, and his thoughts. The rest of him had
> disappeared.... There was nothing to help him – not his
> money, his car, his father's reputation, his suit or his
> shoes. In fact, they hampered him. (p. 280)

(Ironically, as Milkman endures this ritualistic "molting" in a Southern forest, in Detroit, Hagar, in a final bid for his affection, is frantically grasping after clothes and the same types of objects her lover is simultaneously discarding.)

In the hunting episode, Morrison demonstrates, among other things, that man is set off from the other animals by virtue of the gift of reason, and has responsibility to use that gift to the best of his ability. As he wanders in the primordial forest, Milkman finally comes to terms with himself, accepting the components, positive and negative, that contribute to his existence as a complete human being. Self-acceptance makes interrelations with others both possible and meaningful, for only when man ceases to struggle against who and what he is can he live with himself in any semblance of harmony.

In this newly-achieved state of spiritual harmony, Milkman is prepared to accept not only the revelation of truths about himself and his family, but more importantly, he acknowledges responsibility for what his life has been and will be. Morrison demonstrates that this metamorphosis has taken place with the scene wherein Milkman is confronted with the guilt of his role in causing Hagar's death. Recalling the words of his grandfather's spirit, "You can't fly on off and leave a body," he decides that he, like Pilate, must abide by their wisdom. His connection with his cousin's death is symbolized by the shoebox filled with the dead woman's hair that becomes Milkman's own "inheritance." Even after he is reconciled with Pilate, who offers to bury the box, he refuses to relinquish it, preferring to keep it as part of his life, just as Hagar herself had been part of his life.

The final indication that Milkman's long apprenticeship to Pilate has been successfully completed appears at the very close of the novel, as Pilate lies dying from a gunshot wound inflicted by Guitar. The expiring woman gives her nephew the same command her father gave her years before: "Sing!" In response, he instinctively sings the same "song of Solomon," which she had sung over thirty years ago, just prior to the insurance man's suicide and Milkman's own birth. Whether the song is viewed as a dirge of death or a hymn to life is irrelevant. What is important is the message, the lesson it commemorates, namely, if the individual is at peace with himself, if he is secure with his image of himself as a just being, there is no obstacle he cannot transcend.

Notes

[1]Abram Kardianer and Lionel Ovesey, The Mark of Oppression (Cleveland: World Publishing Company, 1967), p.70.
[2]Kardiner and Ovesey, p.29.
[3]Gayle, Way of the New World, p.18.
[4]Kardiner and Ovesey, p.8.
[5]E. Franklin Frazier, Black Bourgeoisie: The Rise of a New Middle Class in the United States (New York: Collier Books, 1962), p.26.
[6]Bandler, Toni Morrison, p.28.
[7]Bandler, Toni Morrison, p.28.
[8]Bandler, Toni Morrison, p.28.
[9]Morrison, Song of Solomon, p.231. All quotations will be from this edition.
[10]Frazier, Black Bourgeoisie, p.10.
[11]Lillian Hornstein, G.D. Percy, and Sterling Brown, eds., The Reader's Companion to World Literature (New York: New American Library, 1973), p.183.
[12]Benson, Images, pp.253-54.
[13]Frazier, Black Bourgeoisie, pp.11-13.
[14]Trellie Jeffers, "The Black Black Woman and the Black Middle Class," Black Scholar, March-April 1973, pp.39-40.
[15]Leatha S. Mitchell, "Toni Morrison, My Mother, and Me," in In Memory and Spirit of Frances, Zora and Lorraine, ed Julliette Bowles (Washington, D.C.: Institute for the Arts and Humanities, Howard University, 1979), p.58.
[16]Richard M. Dorson, American Negro Folktales (New York: Fawcett World Library, 1967), p.15.
[17]Benson, Images, p.254.

Chapter 5

THE THIRD LIFE OF GRANGE COPELAND AND MERIDIAN

THE SOUTHERN EXPERIENCE AND

THE EVOLUTION OF BLACK AMERICAN CONSCIOUSNESS

The works of many contemporary black American authors, Ishmael Reed, Shirley Anne Williams, and Ernest Gains among others, attest to the truth of the statement of psychiatrists Abram Kardiner and Lionel Ovesey in the Mark of Oppression, namely, that to an extent, American blacks do indeed share the same "basic personality."[1] Of course, customs vary from one geographic region to the next, so that variance in behavioral norms are bound to occur. The works of Toni Morrison and Alice Walker address the general conditions of blacks in America, but the importance attributed to specific issues will certainly vary as settings change. The personalities of characters who populate Morrison's novels may reflect their Southern heritage in one way or another, but the problems which complicate their lives tend to be indicative of the urban experience of the Northern black.

Walker's novels, set in the South, deal with conditions stemming from the historical developments which have taken place in that area. However, the fact that the South is the spiritual home of the Afro-American makes the experiences of her characters meaningful to all black Americans, regardless of present residence. The Bluest Eye, Sula, and Song of Solomon all commend the spirit of rebellion which prompted many blacks of the late nineteenth and early twentieth centuries to protest the conditions in the South by migrating to the North and other areas of the nation. On the other hand, The Third Life of Grange Copeland (1970) (hereafter referred to as The Third Life) and Meridian (1976), both laud the courage, perseverance, and revolutionary spirit of the men and women who undertook the task of correcting the virulent Southern conditions like lynching and disenfranchisment, which caused the exodus of those pioneers of the preceding generations. Mary Helen Washington heralds Walker as an apologist and chronicler for black women, applauding her "evolutionary treatment of the black woman."[2] While it is true that Walker, a socialist-feminist, does give special attention to the circumstances of the oppressed woman, The Third Life and Meridian are far more than paeans to feminism. Beginning with The Third Life, Walker graphically describes the development of social and political consciousness among Southern blacks from the era of post-Reconstruction (according to the data provided, Grange Copeland is born circa 1885) to the advent of the passively rebellious stage which introduced the revolutionary movement of the 1960's. It is during the latter period that Grange's granddaughter Ruth, the personification of his progressive "third life," comes of age. Walker continues her presentation of the evolution of the black revolution with Meridian, the author's personal interpretation of the response of the middle-class, black, Southern revolutionary to the social, political, and economic plight of the black man in the South. While she closely resembles Toni Morrison in her authentic depiction of the horrors which blight the lives of some black Americans, Walker also bears a very strong likeness to Hermann Kant, and to an extent, to Guenter De Bruyn, for she deliberately outlines the stages of the individual's advance toward self-consciousness and political and social awareness.

Historically, the experience of the Southern black was and still is primarily that of the man of the soil. Agriculture was one of the chief industries of West Africa during the period of European exploration and colonization of the so-called New World. Norman Coombs (The Black Experience in America, 1972) and Stanley M. Elkins (Slavery: Problem in American Institutional and Intellectual Life, 1963) proffer the possibility that the agricultural background of the African might have contributed to his desirability for the praedial slave system which formed the foundation of the plantation economy of the ante-bellum South. Whether or not he had any special affinity for tilling the soil, the African slave and his descendants comprised the majority of the Southern peasant class, and continue as the dominant element of the population of that social segment to this day. In her cultural study of the Deep South, Hortense Powdermaker analyzes the issue of the black peasantry of the South:

The plantation system in our community stems directly from the plantation of the old South. Before the Civil War, the landlord had complete responsibility for the welfare of the slaves who provided the labor.... They had no control over their labor and no direct share in its profits. Money played no part in the dealings between master and workers.... After freedom, there was still the cotton to be planted, cultivated, and picked. There were still the plantations. And there was a set of mores so strongly entrenched that not even a war could dislodge them. The Negro was still the worker. The white man, much poorer than before, still made the decisions. Landlords who had sufficient wealth after the Civil War to continue as planters, translated the responsibility for slaves to responsibility for tenants. Sometimes a man's tenants were the same Negroes who had formerly been his slaves. Many slaves merely transferred their dependence from master to landlord.... Nevertheless, the Negro was free. He had acquired the right to move, even though he had not always been able to exercise that right.[3]

Born in a small town called Eatonton in 1944, Walker was reared in rural Georgia, where she learned first-hand of the experiences of the black plantation worker, later portrayed in her first novel. In an article entitled "My Father's Country Is the Poor,"[4] Walker describes events in the life of her father, a poor laborer who was often exploited by the rural, middle-class rich. The lives of some of her characters bear a striking resemblance to the description she gives of her father's life. Walker's writings also reflect the strong influence of her intellectual mentor, Zora Neale Hurston, who first came to prominence during the Harlem Renaissance of the 1920's. An advocate of black feminism and the "black aesthetic," Hurston makes use of the distinctively black speech patterns, folklore, religious beliefs, and rituals that are also to be found in Walker's works.

The Third Life tells of a family whose situation is practically identical to the dilemma described above by Powdermaker. With the history of three generations of the Copeland family, Walker exposes the evils of a brutal system that contributes heavily to the mental and physical demise of individuals and, at times, of entire families. Despite the severity of the events and conditions depicted in her works, the author insists that the individual should exercise his free will by actively deciding which course of life he will follow. Only thus can he develop spiritually. Naturally, this also implies that each individual must bear the responsibility for the outcome of his actions or omissions.

This novel tells of one man's personal liberation, an experience that not only benefits him, but enables him to assist in the liberation of his posterity. In the prime of his life, Grange Copeland is one generation removed from slavery, and believes his lot in life to be in no way an improvement over that of his enslaved ancestors. His survival, like theirs and that of countless of his immediate peers, depends upon his working the soil - land that is not his own. Through nomenclature, Walker emphasizes the intimate bond existing between the sharecropper and the land. The names Grange, Copeland, and Brownfield all refer to the soil that provides the sharecropper's sustenance, but seemingly holds him prisoner at the same time. Like his forebearers, Grange (and later his son) is beaten down by the prevailing economic and social systems. In turn, he vents the anger and built-up violence provoked by the constant humiliation and frustration he must endure on the only victims less powerful than himself - his wife and child. Though poignantly sympathetic to Grange and those he represents (after all, as Washington points out, many of the characters portrayed in the novel are patterned after figures from the author's own life[5]), Walker never allows her readers to lose sight of the one all-important factor that makes the case of Grange different from that of the slaves. As pointed out by Powdermaker in After Freedom, unlike their ancestors, Grange and Brownfield are free and have the right of choice. They also have the human right of freedom of movement, and although it might be difficult for them to exercise those privileges, the feat would not be impossible. In fact, the refusal to exercise their rights condemns them and those dependent upon them to a continuing life of drudgery.

Grange is well into his first "life," when the novel opens. It is an existence characterized by poverty, resentment, and despair. At the age of thirty-five, he is a husband and father, and a man grown old and worn before his time, having worked his entire life within the framework of a system purposely designed to keep him in debt and thereby enslaved. Consequently, he can provide no tangible evidence to account for any positive accomplishments of his past life, and purpose for the future. Even with wife and child also working, the family barely subsists economically. In a society that requires men to adhere to a prescribed pattern of behavior if they are to be recognized and accorded a measure of respect, he finds his "manhood" refuted on a daily basis. Over a prolonged period of time, Grange's industry and energy turn into feelings of futility and bitterness at being trapped within such a labyrinth of oppression and suffering. In his estimation, every white person represents system-ized oppression and dehumanization. Whereas we quickly recognize that it would be virtually impossible for Grange or any average person in his position to meet the standards set by mainstream America, Grange, who is actually caught up in the entanglements impeding his progress, often finds himself bewildered and never thinks to question the legitimacy of the system itself. Rather, he internalizes the guilt for his imagined inadequacies. Because Grange is unable to admit consciously to himself that he might be inadequate, he searches for a scapegoat. Since the etiquette of Southern race relations would prevent him from venting his pent-up hostilities on the whites, he brutalizes instead those closest to him: Margaret and Brownfield, his wife and son, and Fat Josie the prostitute, his long-time lover. Even after his migration to the North, and the start of his "second life," he does not come to the full realization that it is the system more than the individuals that causes men to prey upon the weak-ness and disadvantage of other individuals. That knowledge Grange acquires only in his later years, when he embarks upon his third life in the role of Ruth's guardian, mentor, and friend.

Raw violence pervades the entire novel. Trudier Harris, a scholar in the area of black feminist literature, devotes an entire article, "Violence In The Third Life of Grange Copeland," to analyzing this theme.[6] She agrees with the conclusions expressed by both Walker's and Morrison's works, namely, that the violent acts committed by blacks are most often perpetrated against other blacks. Such actions are tantamount to self-destruction, and of course, counter-revolutionary. Many of the violent aspects of The Third Life resemble those contained in Morrison's novels so closely in detail, that to eleborate upon them would amount to redundancy. Both authors similarly point out, for instance, that the syndrome of inter-familial abuse often persists from one generation to the next if the factors contributing to the disturbance go unchecked. Since, as I mentioned earlier, some factors of the black American experience do not change from one area to the next, one doesn't find it difficult to understand that the story of Grange and Margaret, which later repeats itself in the experiences of Brownfield and Mem, is practically the same as that of Cholly and Pauline Breedlove, or Boy-Boy and Eva Peace. The three phases of spiritual metamorphosis he undergoes distinguish the protagonist of Walker's first novel from her other characters and those of Morrison. That transition symbolizes character growth and personality development, which is not merely recommended or suggested by the author (as in Morrison's works), but actually takes place within the framework of the novel. Walker shows a similar evolution of character in Meridian as well. Morrison's works often ring with a tone of admonition, as she exhorts the reader to recognize the importance of self-knowledge and self-acceptance. However, we know of only one of her characters, Milkman Dead, who ever successfully achieves a state of self-affirmation after leading the first part of his life being ignorant of himself and his background. Walker, on the other hand, calls upon her audience to meet the same challenges Morrison describes, but her outlook on matters is more positive and her approach to solving problems more encouraging than that of her fellow author. For instance, Grange Copeland's early life follows much the same pattern as that of Jude Greene or Cholly Breedlove. For almost half his lifetime, he has practically no concept of himself, or his intrinsic value as a human being. The self-contempt he feels proves overwhelming. Despite that, he does evolve to higher stages of consciousness, while Morrison's characters, with one exception, do not. Walker has Grange provide his own epitaph: "Think of me when I'm gone as a big rough-looking coward. Who learned to love hisself only after thirty-odd years. And then overdone it."[7] This statement suggests that Walker's writing lacks a certain fatalism that is often present in Morrison's works. Walker not only stresses the importance of self-affirmation, but declares her faith in the ability of the oppressed to achieve this psychological state by depicting in her novels characters who succeed in doing just that. Grange's life is far from easy and often hideously ugly, but the knowledge he acquires during the course of his three stages of development, and the personal growth he undergoes, sustain and uphold him and assist in the spiritual development of his posterity.

The brand of violence that characterizes the "first life" has its roots in self-hatred and psychological impotence. From the outset of the novel, Grange lives with a constant awareness of his inability compete within the system, i.e., to measure up to the standards of the established norm, as it were. The sensation of helplessness sets the general mood of much of the novel as the opening scene depicts the departure of the Copelands' Northern relatives after a brief visit. The mention of the visit serves two purposes: (1) it highlights the penury of the Copelands, which makes the rather average financial standing of their cousins seem like opulence; (2) it tempts Grange northward to the so-called "promised land, "where freedom supposedly flourishes and poverty is unknown. The Copelands' indebtedness is so acute that Grange tries to persuade his wife to prostitution. Factors such as these contribute to the erosion of whatever stability Grange might have had. Outbursts of drunken anger and violent threats result. Assaulting and threatening his wife and son not only alienate Grange from his family, but also establishes a dangerous precedent for Brownfield to follow. At the time the novel opens, the child is ten. Over the period of the next five years, he looks on as his parents become so involved with their own problems and pursuits that they become oblivious to his presence among them. As each partner pursues his or her own interests, the marriage disintegrates and the family collapses.

The figurative and literal loss of both parents, but especially the loss of his mother, is probably the most damaging blow Brownfield suffers during his formative years. The emotional damage resulting from the loss persists for the duration of his life. During his first ten years, the relationship between Brownfield and Margaret reflects love and warmth, a fitting balance for the distant, chilly relationship that exists between father and son. In effect, Margaret is her son's shining star until the pressures of life, especially her knowledge of the long-standing affair between Grange and Fat Josie the prostitute drive here to pursue the same dissolute life as her husband. From that point on, Margaret becomes a distasteful stranger to Brownfield.

Margaret interprets her husband's infidelity as rejection and proof of some personal failing on her part, and her self-contempt grows. Doubt of her own worth sends her into the arms of countless lovers, including the white landlord her husband despises, seeking reassurance of her desirability as a woman. An unwanted, illicit pregnancy is the result of her amorous adventures. Two years following the birth of her "nullius filius," Margaret is deserted by Grange, who moves in with Josie. Shortly thereafter, Margaret poisons herself and her baby, leaving Brownfield to make his way through the world on his own.

Trudier Harris states that it is actually the white power structure that destroys Margaret, who allows herself to be used as its tool.[8] This is an unfair assessment, although there is admittedly some truth in the statement. All oppressed people are victims of the reigning power structure, and as a result of their disadvantaged position, they inevitably experience some degree of discord within their ranks, e.g., disintegration of families or mental and/or physical abuse, etc. Suicide, however, is not the normal method of coping with those problems. Margaret, like many of her sisters, does indeed suffer extreme abuse at her husband's hands, but she behaves as brutally toward herself as he. Like many women from the ranks of the oppressed, she dies a violent death, but because she dies by her own hand, her position differs a great deal from those of most other black women in her situation. In fact, in most black-authored literature, the female black suicide does not occur. (The noted exception to this rule is the tragic mulatto heroine of early black literature: she takes her own life rather than return to a life of bondage.) Since they are the traditional transmitters of life and culture, black women are generally portrayed as keeping a tight grip on life, regardless of how many obstacles might arise.[9] Despite all the hostility between them, there is no doubt that Grange and Margaret do love each other, although their love has become warped with the passing of time and the mounting of pressures, but even if all the emotional bonds joining them had been severed, they still would share the obligation and responsibility toward their offspring. By turning his back on Margaret, Grange also shirks his duty as Brownfield's father. Margaret is no less guilty of child desertion, since she goes to her death intentionally, knowing full well that her actions will leave her child bereft of both parents.

With little knowledge of stable family relations, Brownfield is forced to face the realities of an adult world at the age of fifteen. In time, it becomes apparent that the boy is his father's son in more than name. Many facets of his personality bear a remarkable resemblance to those of his father. In my opinion, Brownfield's role in the novel presents an image of Grange as he would have been had he not evolved beyond the first stage of development. Sharing his father's intense distrust of whites, Brownfield plans to travel northward to avoid being trapped in the same entanglements that had previously spelled disaster for his parents. Like innumerable other literati, including Hermann Kant, Walker readily employs the age-old motif of the wanderer who travels about gleaning wisdom from the experiences of life. Brownfield is a wanderer sidetracked from the pursuit of his destiny when he becomes involved with none other than his father's former paramour, Josie. His involvement with her leads him to give up his plans for making a new life in the North. Instead, he contents himself with the position of resident stud for Josie and her daughter. Brownfield, like his mother, makes the mistake of subordinating his independence and individuality to the will of another. The first of a long line of subsequent surrenders, this action indicates that he has voluntarily cast aside his dreams of freedom. At the age of seventeen, two years after coming to Josie, Brownfield marries her niece, Mem, a shy and gentle school teacher. He turns to sharecropping as a temporary means of support. However, the system is not designed to give "temporary" support to anyone. In effect, Brownfield, of his own accord, walks into the trap he had resolved to avoid years before. From this stage in his life, he begins to re-live the episodes of his father's first life.

The marriage of Brownfield and Mem follows almost exactly the same course as that of Grange and Margaret. Like her mother-in-law before her, Mem subordinates her will to that of her husband. Their happiness is shortlived, as the hardships and pressures of survival sour Brownfield's spirits after a few years. By the time his elder children are four and five years of age, their father has succeeded in earning their fear and disgust. It is around this time that his marriage crumbles once he returns to the affections and ministrations of Josie. He loses that haven when Grange returns unexpectedly from New York and marries Josie, thus permanently cementing the barrier that had separated him from his son for so many years. The single positive event of that period is the birth of Ruth, Brownfield's youngest daughter and the symbol of her grandfather's third life.

The failure of Brownfield Copeland's life can be attributed to his personal failings as well as the harshness of the system under which he lives. I base this conclusion upon the following observations. First, we recall that Brownfield consciously elects to give up his dream of freedom in order to enjoy the "good life" of servicing Josie and her daughter, Lorene. Second, instead of seeking a new life with his bride, Brownfield commits himself to a system he knows to be thoroughly corrupt - in short, he walks open-eyed into the grip of oppression. Third, as the novel progresses, it becomes quite obvious that Brownfield indulges in violence simply because he enjoys inflicting pain. In this aspect, he differs from his father, for although Grange does indulge in brutal acts, he also shows signs of repentance. Brownfield never does. The life of the son is no harder than his father's had been; yet the "revenge" he seeks for the wrongs committed against him is monstrous. What injustice perpetrated against him by the system could inspire any rational man to deliberately deprive his family of decent housing, to murder his helpless, infant son by exposing him to the freezing elements, or to shoot down his wife before the eyes of his children! Brownfield's senseless, vicious actions damage the psyche of a third generation of Copelands, ensuring the persistence of the syndrome of self-contempt and ego-obliteration.

The particulars of the "second life" of Grange Copeland are revealed only after the third life actually commences. Consuming hatred also characterizes Grange's second life. Instead of directing the emotions of contempt toward himself, however, Grange aims them at what he considers a more suitable target, the white world. During his sojourn in the North, he finally learns that it is suicidal for the oppressed to automatically accept the "correctness" of the status quo, since such acceptance is the same as self-condemnation. During an interview conducted by Mary Helen Washington, Walker discloses that all of her life, she has known people who lack a sense of self. She recalls that her own mother once commented that she believed whites to be "just naturally smarter, prettier, and better than all other people."[10] Firmly rejecting such an attitude, Walker leaves no doubt that she condemns all inclinations toward ego-obliteration and personality defacement. She portrays the brutal confrontation between Grange and a pregnant white girl, that results in the girl's death and his "conversion" to the creed of "love thyself and hate thine enemy." The girl's death gives Grange a certain exhilirating freedom and convinces him that only stark hatred of the oppressor can ensure the survival of the oppressed:

> "Teach them to hate!" he shouted up and down the Harlem streets, his eyes glazed with his new religion. "Teach them to hate if you wants them to survive!" ... "Hatred for them will someday unite us," he shouted from the corner of Seventh Avenue. "It will be the only thing that can do it. Deep in our hearts we hates them anyhow. What I say is brang it out in the open and teach it to the young 'uns. If you teach it to them young, they won't have to learn it in the school of hard knocks." (pp. 153-54)

At this stage in his life, Grange's outlook on the political situation resembles the creed professed by the Black Muslims and other separatist groups. The white man was seen as evil personified, the "blue-eyed devil," who by his very nature merited the hatred and contempt of all other peoples. For a short while after his conversion, Grange revels in his new-found belligerence, fighting every white he encounters, venting the frustrations of a lifetime. Eventually overtaken by the realization that he cannot "punish" the entire white world, he retreats into a world of his own making, where whites have no place. He expresses his belief in this particular kind of separatism as he argues with Brownfield about the misdeeds of their mutual past. "I don't have to admit a damn thing to you," said Brownfield, "and I ain't about to let the crackers off the hook for what they done to my life." "I'm talking to you, Brownfield," said Grange, "and most of what I'm saying is you got to hold tight a place in you where they can't come.... We keep killing ourselves for peoples that don't even mean nothing to us!" (p.209) Although his inclination toward pugilism declines, Grange's hatred for the white race diminishes only with the passing of time, but never completely disappears. Had his last years not been spent in close association with his granddaughter, Ruth, it is highly doubtful that Grange would have undergone the transition from the second to the third stage of character development. Even though the mental attitude that he develops during the second phase of his life is healthier than its precedessor, it is not possible to say that he has achieved a state of psychological balance since he is an individual who is consumed by hatred. Walker comments, "I have found in my own writing that a little hatred, keenly directed, is a useful thing."[11] In this statement, the author admits feeling that even hatred need not be totally negative if it is only moderately employed; however, the individual who does indulge in the use of hatred as a psychological crutch or implement must be ever-aware of the possibility of over indulgence. Just as hatred plays a leading role in the first two lives of Grange Copeland, it also pervades the third, although not as the same wild and destructive passion of previous times. The hatred which is evidenced in Grange's third life has been honed by his new-found responsibilities and tempered by the love he feels for his new charge. Responsibility for Ruth brings Grange to the realization that love is a tool that can be just as effective, and certainly healthier for the human psyche, as hatred. He discovers, "... with Ruth he had learned an invaluable lesson about hate: he could only teach hate by inspiring it.... At least love was something that left a man proud that he had loved. Hate left a man shamed, as he was now, before the trust and faith of the young." (p. 157)

As mentioned earlier, the works of Zora Neale Hurston exercise a stark influence upon Alice Walker. An advanced acolyte in the study of voodoo, Hurston makes many references to root medicine and the art of conjure in her fiction. Ellease Southerland points out that a system of numerology is one of the first expressions of voodoo influences to appear in Hurston's works.[12] Southerland goes on to point out that for devotees of voodoo, the number three has a special meaning; namely, it symbolizes the conclusion or culmination of things. In a manner reminiscent of her intellectual forebearer, Walker draws upon her own knowledge of numbers to emphasize certain facts. Because The Third Life is intended to celebrate the conclusion of an era marred by hatred and a lack of hope, the use of the number three recurs throughout the novel: (1) Grange Copeland is thrice metamorphosized; (2) Ruth, the instrument of her grandfather's salvation, as it were, belongs to the third generation of Copelands appearing in the novel; (3) as the daughter of Mem and the granddaughter of Margaret, Ruth represents the third stage of development in feminist consciousness discussed herein; (4) the third surviving child of Brownfield and Mem, Ruth is the only one with hopes of having a meaningful future, since Daphne is committed to an asylum and Ornette becomes a prostitute. As the youngest of the three, Ruth comes under her grandfather's care at an early age so that the effects of Brownfield's mental and physical badgering can be at least partially reversed.

Mem's death and Brownfield's imprisonment for her murder trigger the start of the "third life," by consigning Ruth and her sisters to the custody of their grandfathers. The elder girls go with Mem's father to New York City, where they eventually succumb to the psychological injuries inflicted upon them by their father. Ruth clings to Grange who resolves to save her from what seems to have become the tragic fate of too many Copelands. The relationship between Grange and Ruth is one of responsibility and love. It is the primary theme of the "third life." The portrayal of this relationship is the author's dream of unity and collaboration among members of every representative group within the ranks of the oppressed. This representation symbolizes the synthesis of the old and the new, the radical and the moderate, of hatred and love. It highlights the evolutionary nature of revolution by demonstrating how the gains of each generation rests upon the foundations laid by its predecessors, and at the same time, stresses that that which is already established must be re-fortified on occasion. Grange strives to make his charge the object of his love and the heir to his wisdom, but he openly acknowledges that she, in her turn, matches his own generosity in giving of herself. In "My Father's Country Is the Poor," which was written shortly after her return from a visit to Cuba, Walker notes that socially progressive countries encourage communal education of the entire population as a means of fostering respectful communication between all age groups. By representing Grange and Ruth as she does, the author reasserts her belief in the potential of the grass roots Southern black revolutionary and her faith in the ultimate triumph of the oppressed.

The Third Life brings the reader only as far as the opening of the decade of the sixties, which heralds the escalation of the Civil Rights Movement. The novel closes at this point with the lifelong conflict between Brownfield and Grange reaching its zenith in a legal battle for the custody of sixteen-year-old Ruth, and culminating in the death of both father and son. Realistically, the author has no choice other than to end the novel at this point if verisimilitude is to be preserved. Ruth, who during her formative years represents a stage of development in her grandfather's life, eventually reaches a level of maturity that compels her to strike out for her own intellectual independence if she is to achieve her fullest potential. With her maturation comes the figurative end of the "third life" of Grange Copeland and the end of an era, with the old making way for the new.

As I mentioned earlier, The Third Life concerns itself primarily with the liberation of specific individuals. Although the intrinsic value of the individual is understood, acknowledged, and indeed stressed in the works of Walker and Morrison, the revolutionary artist is interested in the liberation of the individual as a factor affecting the general well-being of the people as a whole. In The Third

Life, Walker does not discuss the Civil Rights Movement in great
detail or depth. She mentions it just enough to suggest that Ruth,
the symbol of the future, is at least aware that the status quo can
be challenged and the established norm altered. Published six years
after The Third Life, Meridian, Walker's second novel, picks up
from the point at which the earlier works closes. It acquaints the
reader with the Civil Rights Movement from its earliest years. A
socio-political coalition which swept through the nation, the Civil
Rights Movement challenged the system and challenged all blacks to
decide whether they were willing to continue their lives as a sup-
pressed, subjugated people, or whether to strike out and demand
all the rights of citizenship guaranteed by the Constitution. The
Movement serves as the pivotal point around which the action of the
novel revolves, because the major theme of the work is the struggle for dominance between the values of the old order and the new.
The entire novel eulogizes those reformers whose struggle to secure freedom and justice for the masses of oppressed, at the expense of their own comfort, security, and lives, shook the foundations of the American political and social system in the 1960's and
1970's.

Meridian is the story of the quest of one woman, who seeks identity
and the right to "become," that is, to develop to the fullest potential
possible. That woman, Meridian Hill, emerges as the middle-class
counterpart of Grange Copeland. Though they belong to different social classes and hail from different backgrounds, they share the experience of undergoing an intense, spiritual metamorphosis (which
Walker calls a distinct life) before finding a meaningful place in
society. In many ways, the early life of Meridian Hill calls to mind
the situation of Milkman Dead. As children from middle-class black
families, these two characters belong to a social order that jeal-
ously guards its "elevated" standing by constantly reminding its
members of the uniqueness that distinguishes them from the common
fold. As mentioned in an earlier chapter, however, the black bourgeoisie suffers from an especially devastating type of alienation and
identity crisis, because it has divorced itself from its ethnic roots.
By analyzing Meridian's life, Walker brings to light the dilemma of
thousands of middle-class black youth who participated in the Move-

ment. (Like most modern revolutions, the Black Revolution of the 1960's had its roots in the sufferings of the poor and oppressed, but was actually put into motion through the efforts ot those "radical" students and intellectuals who themselves belonged to the middle classes.)

Surrounding the first phase of Meridian's life, her formative years, as it were, is an aura of distance and vacuousness. The results of loveless or sterile home situations such as those that scar the personalities of characters like Morrison's Macon and Ruth Dead, or De Bruyn's Karl and Elisabeth Erp, do not leave the Hill family unscathed. The behavior of Meridian's parents, and to an extent, that of the heroine herself, point to some forms of psychological imbalance. The outward appearance of the home environment might suggest calm contentment and stability, but beneath the surface, the situation is anything but idyllic. Headed by a compassionate but defeated father and a bitter, limited mother, the Hill household is totally devoid of any outward displays of love or affection. Like Morrison, Walker attaches an almost mystical quality to the relationship enjoyed by mother and child and demonstrates throughout the novel that the failures of Meridian's mother, who represents the old order of the status quo, contribute to the psychological damage her daughter suffers.

A former teacher, Mrs. Hill has an exaggerated sense of her position as an educator among a group of people, who two to three generations earlier were denied the privilege of literacy. In fact, she bears a striking resemblance to Macon Dead II, who is also an outstanding "self-made success." A woman who married and bore children for the wrong reasons (she felt she was missing something even the lowliest woman enjoyed), she harbors a deep-seated grudge toward her family and society in general for "cheating" her of her independence. Her only valued possessions are her sense of propriety and her imagined "standing" in the community, which she protects at all cost. Though dissatisfied with her life, Mrs. Hill continues with the charade she believes expected of her and tries to force her family to conform in like manner. In her bitterness, she subconsciously punishes them for the disappointments life has meted out to her. Love and approval are withheld, and surrendered only when her conditions are met. She manipulates her husband and children by preying upon a false sense of guilt that plagues them all. Worst of all, her children, especially her daughter, are not allowed to benefit from the knowledge the mother has gleaned from past experiences. Walker seems to believe that Mrs. Hill withholds the information for two reasons: (1) to divulge certain facts would not be in keeping with the image she has of herself as a middle-class matron; (2) a certain subconscious spitefulness leads her to begrudge Meridian any opportunity that she herself did not have:

> When her children were older and not so burdensome - and they were burdens to her always - she wanted to teach again but could not pass the new exams and did not like the new generation of students.... She never learned to cook well, she never learned to braid hair prettily or to be in any other way creative in her home. She could have done so, if she had wanted to. Creativity was in her, but it was refused expression. It was all deliberate. A war against those to whom she could not express her anger or shout, "It's not fair!"...
> With her own daughter she certainly said things she herself did not believe. She refused to help and seemed, to Meridian, never to understand. But all along she understood perfectly. It was for stealing her mother's serenity, for shattering her mother's emerging self, that Meridian felt guilty from the very first, though she was unable to understand how this could possibly be her fault.[13]

It would seem that Walker casts Mrs. Hill in a role similar to Brownfield Copeland's, that is, as a parent given to bruising the psyche of his offspring in an effort to be revenged upon the system that "ruined" his life. By surrendering to her vengeful emotions, Mrs. Hill puts her services at the disposal of the same system she claims to resent. The detriment of her deliberate neglect is just as serious as Brownfield's physical abuse. By intentionally keeping Meridian in a state of ignorance, she denies her the chance for a better life. Such omissions serve only to perpetuate the general ignorance in which oppression is rooted.

Walker devotes relatively little attention to Meridian's father, who like his wife, is certainly not to be celebrated as a revolutionary image. While she praises him as an intelligent, compassionate humanitarian, the author is quick to point out that he is also a defeated man, resigned to accepting whatever fate seems to hand him. His single fixation, an obsession with the historical plight of the American Indian, causes Walker to praise him, but also stimulates her curiosity about a man who emphathizes with people long dead, but seems oblivious to the suffering of his contemporaries, whom he sees on a daily basis. Perhaps his obsession with the dead is a symbol that Mr. Hill has died to the world around him.

Having grown up under the influence of two such parents, it is small wonder that Meridian, in her first life, shows signs of the same mental stagnation that afflicts her mother. Impregnated, married, deserted and divorced before reaching the age of eighteen, she has found life a burden before she has had the opportunity to savor some of its beauty, and there is little prospect for a more promising future. In this respect, Meridian is representative of the majority of talented black youth, who prior to the sixties, faced the prospect of leading limited, unfulfilled lives. The novel conveys the message that Walker considers every individual an artist. She deplores the social, political, or economic system that denies the individual the right to give expression to his art, whatever its nature. In her own words, the result of such a denial is cruel enough to "stop the blood."[14] The arrival of a group of Civil Rights workers in Meridian's hometown changes her life, perhaps even preserves her sanity, by making her aware of her God-given right to pursue a lifestyle different from that which she has traditionally regarded as her own. Her involvement with and deepening commitment to the Movement necessitates bringing her first life to an end in order to pursue a more positive future.

The concept of revolution does not imply denial of the past, but rejection of what progressive thinkers regard as the decadent values of the old order. Meridian is dotted with flashbacks of the protagonist's past (so many, in fact, that we sometimes lose our perspective of time), to impress us with the degree of influence the past wields over her. Walker emphasizes the past to stress that revolution is indeed an evolutionary process that is built upon the incidents of the past and to indicate the enormity of the task undertaken by those like Meridian, who rejected the security of the past to plod ahead into areas that were hostile as well as unfamiliar.

Meridian's efforts to contribute to the Movement earn the disapproval and scorn of her mother, as might be expected; but it also attracts the notice of Northern philanthropists, whose offer to finance the girl's college education brings mother and daughter into dire conflict. Pursuit of higher education would entail Meridian's placing her child up for adoption, an action Mrs. Hill condemns as immoral. (She, however, does not offer to take her grandchild herself.) Despite all logical explanations, the older woman spitefully castigates her daughter, exploiting the guilt she herself is responsible for instilling. It is totally irrelevant to her that without more training, Meridian will be unable to care for herself or the child. This confrontation between mother and daughter calls to mind Michelle Wallace's comment that the image of the indestructable, larger-than-life black mother, the "black superwoman," as it were, does not represent a positive ideal for black womanhood. To celebrate an image which limits the black female to the role of motherhood alone would be counter-revolutionary, since that would deny the individual's right to evolve to her greatest potential and highest level of consciousness. It would, in fact, serve to bolster paternalism to which revolution is diametrically opposed.

Meridian ultimately persists in following the dictates of her own conscience, but her mother's barrage of accusations and maledictions is not ineffectual in the least. In addition to aggravating the guilt complex she has borne for years, the final confrontation brings about the advance of a degenerative nervous disorder that continues to paralyze Meridian until she finally loses ties with all the obstructions of her first life. This physical affliction, characterized by the loss of weight and thinning hair, persists over a period of years and symbolizes a rite of purification. Each attack and subsequent recovery signifies a gradual "dying" to the values of the capitalistic system. However, the reader does not come to realize this until Meridian is well into her second phase of development.

Walker states in an interview that "coming to the end of a cycle means understanding something through to completion. "[15] Meridian's resolve to complete her education signals the close of her first life by indicating that she has come to recognize and thereby reject the narrow confines of a life of ignorance and poverty. Using Meridian as her mouthpiece, Walker declares that "revolution begins not with acts of violence and destruction, but with teaching and understanding. " (p. 188) It is significant then that Meridian's second life begins at the same time as her career as a university student. Her first year at Saxon College is an academic success, but a spiritual failure. Her justification for giving up her son had been that higher education would give her a second chance to find a menaingful life. She realizes that what she had failed to admit, even to herself, at the time the scholarship was offered to her was that it could provide an avenue of escape from her mother and her primeval burden of guilt and unworthiness, as well as a reprieve from a life of poverty and ignorance. The refusal to confront and analyze her situation candidly places Meridian at the disadvantage of being a fugitive from her own conscience. Certain events of her freshman year make it clear beyond a doubt that a change of physical environment has not altered Meridian's psychological state, since the psychological pressures she experiences have not changed; that is, the administration of the college embraces and fosters the same pretentions she seeks to escape by leaving her hometown and her mother's influence. For example, like Mrs. Hill, the administrators of Saxon College profess to set great store by the virtues of Christianity, so much that the student body is required to attend general prayer meetings on a daily basis. Yet, they deny burial to an innocent child because they hesitate to offend the middle-class sense of propriety. Meridian cannot reconcile herself to the hypocrisy that runs rampant at Saxon:

> The emphasis at Saxon was on form, and the preferred "form" was that of the finishing school girl whose goal, wherever she would later find herself in the world, was to be accepted as an

equal because she knew and practiced all the proper social
rules.... A saying about Saxon was that you could do anything
there, as long as you wore spotless white gloves.... (p. 95)

Although her sense of integrity is offended, the fear of appearing
ungrateful prevents her from giving vent to the outrage pent up inside. A more subtle reason for her hesitation to protest is that she
subconsciously identifies Saxon with her mother, since both represent authority figures which espouse the code of the black bourgeoisie. She equates rejection of Saxon with rejection of her mother,
and in her own words, it is death not to love one's mother (p. 30).
In her sophomore year, Meridian is forced to acknowledge her ivory
tower image of Saxon and her delusions for attending the institution.
She joins the Atlanta Movement in that same year, Walker writes,
because "she found it impossible to study while others were being
beaten and jaled." (p. 94) There is undoubtedly an element of humani-
tarianism in her motives. However, I believe that Meridian's involvement in the Movement is a type of mental flagellation, a means of as-
suaging the everpresent guilt that manifests itself in the form of mi-
graine headaches and fits of manic depression. Meridian regards the
protesters' confrontations with the police and ensuing beatings and
imprisonment as a means of release from the mental torments that
relentlessly hound her: "Only during a crisis could she forget. While
other students dreaded confrontation with the police, she welcomed
it, and was capable of an inner gaiety, a sense of freedom, as she
saw the clubs slashing down on her from above." (p. 97)

In her role as a revolutionary artist, Walker is intent upon teaching
her own theory of revolution through the medium of her art. She constructs Meridian in a manner that forces the issues of revolution.
What distinguishes the revolutionary from the reactionary? Do the
aims of the revolution supersede the value of human life and humani-
tarianism in importance? How are the concepts of identity and self-
affirmation related to that of revolution? As the drama of Meridian's
second life unfolds, Walker points out that the individual who has not
considered such questions cannot possibly grasp the meaning and significance of revolution. Meridian's primary goal in her second life is
not only to strengthen her commitment to the revolution, but to perfect her understanding of it, thereby reinforcing her loyalty automatically.

Unlike The Third Life, which merely hints at Walker's socialist leaning, Meridian voices outright both the author's abhorrence of capitalism and her belief that the old order will give way as the revolution progresses. Walker indicates that sincere commitment to change is a fundamental prerequisite of every true revolutionary. However, it is the nature of the change that determines whether it is truly revolutionary. Anne-Marion Coles, Meridian's college roommate, and Truman Held, with whom the protagonist has a short-lived love affair, are "ardent" followers of the Civil Rights Movement; yet Walker uses them to represent the reactionary forces at work within the novel. The relationships Meridian has with these two characters are devastatingly painful, but also enlighteningly educative, since they bring Meridian to the point of analysis and confrontation. The protagonist's interactions with these two characters emphasize that revolution is successful only if it takes place in the minds of the people.

The outward veneer of Anne-Marion and Truman first causes them to appear to be the charismatic characters Meridian imagines. Since she is basically insecure in her position at Saxon, Meridian feels flattered by the attention of individuals who present the image of a revolutionary. They wear the right clothes, work with the Movement (for whatever reasons), and regurgitate the "proper" revolutionary rhetoric. Unfortunately, Meridian does not learn until a great deal of time has elapsed and quite a bit of pain has been endured, that the revolutionary spirit of Anne-Marion and Truman is as superficial as the outward trappings they don. The two of them represent those individuals who equate freedom with tolerance and justice with acceptance based upon outward form. For them, the Civil Rights Movement is essentially a weapon with which to challenge the white man's virility, financial standing, and basic power structures. Equality and justice mean the right to have what the white man has and to do what he does. Since Anne-Marion and Truman reason along these lines, it is inevitable that each will "discard" Meridian when the relationship with her is no longer an asset or becomes an affront the vision each has of himself/herself as a just person. Anne-Marion professes a deep hatred for capitalism and profound devotion to the revolution that could even inspire her to kill for its causes. Her actions later disclose that she has a false concept of the nature of oppression and of revolution, and that she has no idea of what revolution should bring about. What annoys her is that she knows that Meridian, supposedly the unsophisticated rustic, is all that she, Anne-Marion, should be. Walker points out the difference between the two:

> Both girls had lived and studied enough to know they despised capitalism; they perceived it had done well in America because it had rested directly on their fathers' and mothers' backs. The difference between them was this: Anne-Marion did not know if she would be a success as a capitalist, while Meridian did not think she could enjoy owning things others did not have. Anne-Marion wanted blacks to have the same opportunity to make as much money as the richest white people. But Meridian wanted the destruction of the rich as a class and the eradication of all personal economic reserves. . . . Anne-Marion thought this was quaint. When black people can own the seashore, she said, I want miles and miles of it. And I never want to see a face I didn't invite walking across my sand. Meridian reminded her of her professed admiration for socialist and communist theories. Yes, Anne-Marion replied. I have the deepest admiration for them, but since I haven't had a chance to have a capitalist fling yet, the practice of those theories will have to wait awhile. But Anne-Marion, Meridian would say, that is probably exactly what Henry Ford said! Tell Henry I agree with him, said Anne-Marion. These exchanges would be marked by laughter and the attempt to pretend they were not serious. (p. 118)

When Meridian's presence becomes too great an irritant for Anne-Marion's conscience to bear, the latter simply discards her friend, despite the closeness of past ties.

Meridian's relationship with Truman addresses the issue of revolution and sexual politics, and briefly examines the phenomenon of paranoia that developed in some black women after black men began to openly seek out white women.

Truman Held looks on the denial of civil rights as the denial of his "manhood." The racially oppressed man who places a premium on masculinity all too often regards the female of his own race as a mere reflection of his personal oppression. Unfortunately, Truman is such a man at the time of his involvement with Meridian. She exists only for his pleasure.

When the new liberalism of the sixties sanctions interracial unions – usually comprised of a black male and a white female – Truman takes advantage of the opportunity to "improve" his standing. Meridian is casually replaced by Lynne, the white exchange student Truman eventually marries. Meridian is the "African Queen," upon whom Truman would like to bestow the honor of "bearing his black babies." Lynne, however, is his baton of victory, the symbol that proclaims his equality with the white man, since now, he too possesses a white woman.

Truman displays very little regard for the basic humanity of either of these women. He reads DuBois and Mao, and proclaims the revolution. However, the "change" that occurs in his life comes in the guise of a false state of mind.

Black author Stephen Henderson declares that the road to self-knowledge is the road to regeneration.[16] Along with the pain of discovery, Meridian's dealings with Anne-Marion and Truman bring to the protagonist an insight into her own soul. This incident is tantamount to the phenomenon Henderson names a "baptism of blackness," in Meridian's case, a rejection of the white, middle-class values that had been part of her life for so long, affirmation of black self-hood, destruction of any obstacle to self-hood, and the celebration of blackness.[17] Recognition of self-worth means an automatic remission of the guilt and depression that have weighed upon her for years. It means the release of her spirit. Meridian is brought to the full realization that revolution in its purest sense does not harm human life; it enhances it. More importantly, she learns that only those who understand the difference between the two – harm and enhancement – can ever hope to make revolution a lasting reality.

Notes

[1]Abram Kardiner and Lionel Ovesey, The Mark of Oppression (Cleveland: World Publishing Company, 1967), p. 8.

[2]Mary Helen Washington, "An Essay on Alice Walker, " in Sturdy Black Bridges, ed. Roseann P. Bell, Betty J. Parker, and Beverly Guy-Sheftall (Garden City: Anchor Press/Doubleday, 1979), p. 137.

[3]Hortense Powdermaker, After Freedom (New York: Viking Press, 1939), p. 80.

[4]Alice Walker, "My Father's Country is the Poor, " Black Scholar, Summer 1977, pp. 41-48.

[5]Washington, p. 136.

[6]Trudier Harris, "Violence in The Third Life of Grange Copeland, " College Language Association Journal 19 (1975), pp. 238-47.

[7]Alice Walker, The Third Life of Grange Copeland (New York: Harcourt, Brace Jovanovich, 1970), p. 157. (All quotations taken from this edition.)

[8]Harris, p. 42.

[9]Jeanne-Marie A. Miller, "Images of Black Women in Plays by Black Playwrights, " College Language Association Journal 22 (1977), p. 507.

[10]Washington, Essay, p. 135.

[11]Alice Walker, "The Unglamorous but Worthwhile Duties of the Black Revolutionary Artist or ... of the Black Writer who Simply Works and Writes, " Black Collegian, Sept. -Oct. 1971, p. 5.

[12]Ellease Southerland, "The Influence of Voodoo on the Fiction of Zora Neale Hurston, " in Sturdy Black Bridges, ed. Roseann P. Bell, Bettey J. Parker, and Beverly Guy-Sheftall (Garden City: Anchor Press/Doubleday, 1979), pp. 172-73.

[13]Alice Walker, Meridian (New York: Pocket Books, 1979), p. 50. (All quotations taken from this edition.)

[14]Alice Walker, "In Search of our Mother's Gardens, " Ms., May 1974, p. 65.

[15]Washington, Interview in Sturdy Black Bridges, p. 146.

[16]Mercer Cook and Stephen Henderson, The Militant Black Writer (Madison: University of Wisconsin Press, 1969), p. 72.

[17]Cook and Henderson, p. 95.

Chapter 6

SOCIALIST HUMANISM VERSUS SOCIALIST REALISM
AS THE MAJOR THEME OF KANT'S DIE AULA

In his Frühe Schriften, Karl Marx warns that the individual is in
danger of being lost in a mass society - a society which, as it grows
in size and becomes more mechanized, refuses to acknowledge the
thoughts, desires and needs of the individual, thus contributing to
the process of dehumanization. This mutilation of spirit comes about
as the result of the alienation of the individual from his "self," his
work, and other individuals who make up society. Moreover, Marx
sees this alienation as a weapon, deliberately wielded by one segment of society to achieve its personal ends at the expense of those
less fortunate. In his later, more mature writing, Marx would identify this deliberate attempt at alienation as an aspect of class struggle.

As stated earlier, the individual's sense of identity and worth is effective in determining the role he assumes in society, just as society is instrumental in influencing the indivudual's sense of identity
and worth. It is apparent that deliberate alienation is a means of
control, because it allows the individual's concept of "self" to be
influenced or manipulated to too great an extent by someone other
than himself. Marxist theory attaches great importance to the concept of alienation, making the discussion of any Marxist society incomplete without reference to it. This is significantly true of the
German Democratic Republic, which partially owes its existence
to the severance of the former German republic into eastern and
western sectors, and the course of events between 1945 and 1949
that led to the establishment of two separate German states.[1] The
political ideology of the German Democratic Republic would judge
both of these to be actions deliberately perpetrated by the adherents
of capitalism in an effort to alienate one segment of the German
people from the other.

The partitioning of Germany upon the defeat of the Hitler forces is readily explained to students today. It is, however, more complex to explain or comprehend the coexistence of two separate German states, which share the same background and cultural heritage, and yet are firmly entrenched in different spheres of world politics. The East German view of this juxtaposition of political ideologies is best understood if the historical factors leading to World War II are reviewed.

The historical and psychological impact of the first World War upon Germany was tremendous. In 1919, following the Bolshevik Revolution and the loss of the war, the growth of socialism in Germany steadily gained momentum and was halted only by the rise of fascism. The defeat in war, coupled with the resulting national debts of reparation, the political insecurities of the Weimar Republic, the inflation of the 1920's and the great depression of the 1930's were the basic circumstances fostering the conditions that gave rise to the power of the Nationalsozialistische Deutsche Arbeiterpartei or Nazi Party in Germany. With the German middle class impoverished and countless workers unemployed, the national situation was one of crisis, to which Adolf Hitler responded. Promises of prosperity and the restoration of Germany's former greatness through the establishment of a "Third Reich" aided Hitler in obtaining the votes needed to bring the Nazi Party to power in 1933. Nazism or National Socialism, as it was called, attracted followers from every walk of life, but notedly important was its influence on the contingent composed of the petty bourgeoisie. Using mass psychology, the Nazis were able to maintain a grip on workers and small businessmen, the so-called "kleine Menschen." While simultaneously courting wealthy corporate firms, they were able to divert the anti-corporate sentiments of the small, independent business groups into feelings of anti-Semitism and ultra-nationalism. Kurt F. Reinhardt makes the following observation about Germany under the Nazi regime:

> While all civil and human rights were totally abrogated, all duties and responsibilities converged in the Fuehrer, the embodiment of Volk and Reich.... The Nuernberg Laws eliminated all Jews from the political, economic and cultural life of the German Volksgemeinschaft.... Freedom was pro-

mised to all religious creeds "as far as they do not endanger or are in conflict with the moral ideas of the German race. "[2]

In his novel, Das Beil von Wandsbek ("The Ax of Wandsbek"), Arnold Zweig, who emigrated to East Berlin in 1948, gives a very effective demonstration of how well the Nazis understood the mentality of the "kleiner Mensch." Using extensive detail, Zweig depicts the sharp stratification of German society, and the awareness of the individual with regard to his station in that society: the greater one's material wealth, the higher one's station, which meant, naturally, a greater sense of self-esteem and positive self-image. The fear of falling to the position of blue-collar worker was the nightmare of ultimate degradation for the member of the petit bourgeoisie. Zweig masterfully depicts the strategy employed by the Nazi leadership to successfully deceive the vast majority of Germans by capitalizing on socialist and nationalist trends popularized by the pressures of the post-World War I years. The ultra-conservative, capitalistic nature of Nazism was concealed by representing the NSDAP as the people's party. Preserving some of the standards of Junkerism, the Prussian code favoring the privileged, militaristic, landowning class, Nazism fostered the imperialistic drive which led to the invasion of Poland in September 1939, and the outbreak of the second World War. Six years later, Germany's unconditional surrender resulted in the loss of her territories east of the Oder and Neisse Rivers, and the partitioning of the remaining territory. The former Reich was divided into four occupied zones, each governed exclusively by one of the conquering Allied forces. At the Potsdam Conference of 1945, the Allies agreed to preserve the unity of Germany (especially the economic unity). However, the autonomy of each of the governing powers in its designated zone, coupled with the clash of the political ideologies of East and West, prevented the success of the agreement. In 1949, the amalgamation of the western zones and the establishment of a central government administered by Germans heralded the founding of the Federal Republic of Germany (Die Bundesrepublik Deutschland). In the eastern zone, the German Democratic Republic (Die Deutsche Demokratische Republik) was founded in October of the same year.

The transection of a nation resulting in the enforced division of a people is, without a doubt, a form of alienation. The Marxist view of alienation is often compared with the Judaeo-Christian theme of the Fall of Man.[3] According to Marxist and Christian doctrine, mankind undergoes three stages of development:

(1) Period marked by harmony between self and nature (innocence)
(2) Period marked by strife and turmoil (sin)
(3) Period marked by return to the state of perfection (redemption)

The first two stages have been or are in the process of being experienced by man; the third has yet to be realized. Whereas Christian doctrine teaches that man can only regain his lost grace by vanquishing sin, Marxist doctrine holds that universal harmony can return only when the evils of capitalism are vanquished. This analogy, and the Communist view that sees Nazism as an outgrowth of the socio-economic form of capitalism aid in understanding the socialist perception of the events following in the aftermath of World War II, particularly the political and economic severance of East from West Germany.[4] The socialist Anschauung maintains that the imperialism, nationalism, and militarism, which by necessity accompany capitalism, were responsible for both World Wars. For the majority of East Germans, the roots of the present division of Germany are historically evident as early as 1933, when by voting for or against Hitler, the German nation made a decision to favor or reject fascism. In the official East German view, it is not 1945, but 1933 which marks the turning point in German history.[5]

The establishment of a West German state under western - capitalist - control is interpreted as the intentional restoration of those powers originally liable for the nation's present predicament, i. e. , its division. From the East German perspective, the division was a move on the part of the West to gain another capitalist appendage and an attempt to estrange one segment of German society from the other. Such a move would help ensure the perpetuation of capitalism in West Germany, and was, therefore, soundly condemned by socialist East Germany.

Over the past thirty years, the German Democratic Republic, a nation with a mission, has become acutely aware of its historical role and function as the first socialist state on German territory. This official view has contributed to the growth of a special political and social awareness among the East German citizenry, which is expressed in all the arts, but particularly in that nation's literature.[6]

Afro-Americans, like the East Germans, have become very much attuned to political consciousness and social awareness over the last three decades. Revolutionary artists from both groups concur in the belief that the arts must respond to the needs of the revolution. However, the obstacles confronting the Afro-American artist and those confronting his East German counterpart are as diverse as the political systems governing the U.S. and the DDR. While it may be true that East Germans and Black Nationalists alike have a common foe in capitalism, it is obvious that variances in political, cultural, and historical background will result in the two groups being confronted with political and sociological problems that differ in some ways. "Sociologically informed criticism can help us to avoid making mistakes about the nature of the works of literature we have before us by throwing light on its function or on the conventions with reference to which certain aspects of it are to be understood."[7] This observation of David Daiches is of crucial importance to the Westerner who undertakes a study of the literature of the German Democratic Republic, or any socialist state for that matter, because the function of the arts in a socialist or communist society differs so drastically from that in capitalist nations. In the German Democratic Republic (hereafter referred to as the DDR), socialism is the key concept for the ideological interpretation of the national political system.[8] To paraphrase Lenin, and later Otto Grotewahl, "the pictorial arts and literature must always be subservient to politics in a socialist society." It stands to reason, therefore, that the arts in the DDR are employed to further the tenets and goals of socialism or to solve or prevent any problems that might threaten the progressive development of the socialist state. By necessity, the literature of the DDR must address current events and reflect the political problems of immediate importance. The concept of "art for art's sake" is vehemently rejected by socialist ideology,

and branded as a carry-over from the "degenerate" bourgeois notion that conceives of art as a luxury-item reserved for the privileged. Contrary to the middle-class ideal, which is elitest in nature, the ideal of the socialist state strives to make the people a-
ware that the intended function of culture within their society is the
education of the populace in general. The importance of the role of
the arts in the DDR is further evidenced by the fact that Article 18
of the National Constitution provides for a cultural policy and en-
dows the Minister for Culture with far more power and responsibility than any comparable West European or American minister.[9]

All the arts in the DDR must meet the criteria set down by the state
censory boards - journalists answer to the Abteilung der Agitation
und Propaganda; television and radio personnel report to the Staat-
liches Rundfunkkomittee - which in turn are responsible to the DDR's
only viable political party, the Sozialistische Einheitspartei Deutsch-
lands, or the SED. In order to safeguard Parteilichkeit (party-line
politics) and support party decisions, only politically reliable candidates are appointed to positions which require work with the mass
media. Because literature must reflect the culturo-political development of the DDR as it is interpreted by the SED, it can also be used
as a medium for tracing the socio-political development of the nation
as seen from the official point of view. For example, the official
writings of the DDR subdivide the historical development of that nation into three periods: (1) the anti-fascist democratic upheaval leading to the establishment of a socialist system, 1945-1949; (2) the
transition from a capitalist to a socialist economic system, using
the Soviet system as a model, 1949-1961; (3) the extensive establishment of socialism, stretching from 1961 to the present time.
These phases also represent stages of the evolutionary process of a
new political system, reflected in the national literature.[10] In 1945,
for instance, the first step toward changing the "sowjetische Besatzungszone" to a socialist state required a purge to rid the system
of all elements of fascism. Since East Germans regarded - and continue to regard - the West German government as the natural heir
of the Third Reich, the DDR literature produced during the period
extending from 1945 to 1949 mirrored the hostilities arising from
the radically different political ideologies of the respective sectors.
This literature, however, had no special national flavor reminis-

cent of the DDR, per se. Following the official founding of the DDR, the literature which emerged thereafter reflected trends in national and international politics. The struggle between the two Germanies was viewed as a confrontation between humanistic socialism and materialistic capitalism, and therefore, the politics, morality, and cultural trends of the West were ardently attacked. Formalism in art and literature was condemned and replaced by the tenets of "socialist realism," a term first coined by Ivan Gronski in 1932 to represent the creative principle which requires artists in socialist societies to interpret life according to party-line politics. Since art is elevated to a position of relative importance in the socialist state, the artist is expected to utilize his creative talents to achieve the ideological goals of socialism, even if that should require rejection of long-cherished traditions.

The greatest task undertaken during the early stages of DDR development was that of Aufbau ("construction"). The entire concept of Aufbau in East Germany was far more complicated than the reconstruction achieved in the West under the auspices of the Marshall Plan, first of all because the DDR lacked such assistance, and secondly, because the sociological and ideological forces in the East called for much more than mere physical construction. The connotation of Aufbau, for the East German, included the forging of a socialist identity and socialist consciousness. In July 1952, the Second Conference of the SED proclaimed the actual "construction of socialism." In the DDR, where the socialist political system extends into and includes all regions of the citizen's social life, there is, ideally, no polarity between state and society, nor between private person and citizen.[11] The goals of the state, and therefore those of the individual who is an integral part of the state, are the following: (1) spreading the ideals of Marxism-Leninism; (2) assisting the individual in the development of full socialist maturity; (3) supporting the leadership of the DDR; (4) suppression of all fascist, capitalist and bourgeois tendencies. Since the major emphasis was placed upon the construction of a socialist society during the period of Aufbau, socialist realism emphasized the working class, which would, of course, be the key factor in making German socialism a reality. The worker and his life, therefore, became the major themes of narrative and prose works. The role of the artist and/or the writer in representing the worker was to bridge the gap between art and life.

Because literature serves a distinct purpose in the DDR, change in literary trends denotes change in the purpose of literature as a medium utilized to spread propaganda. (The term "propaganda" does not carry the negative connotation for the East German citizen as its English or West German counterpart does; rather, it means spreading the ideology of Marxism-Leninism, and has a highly positive function.[12] The foundations of socialism had been laid during the second period of historical development, and the literature of that phase reflects both the economic development of the DDR and the attempts to mold a strong industrial state. Like the literary productions of the first historical period, those of the second portray the West as totally evil and hostile toward the German socialist state. Those feelings of resentment were not unfounded, as the West German government ostracized and isolated the DDR on a world-wide scale during the 1950's and 1960's.[13] For example, for years, the Bundesrepublik (BRD) or Federal Republic refused to even acknowledge the existence of the DDR as a legitimate government; rather, the DDR was referred to as the "sowjetische Besatzungszone," or "Mitteldeutschland," etc., which, for the East German, constituted an insult in addition to indicating that the West would not hesitate to undermine the DDR government, reestablish its own authority, and return to the status quo of the Hitlerzeit. In short, the DDR looked on the policy of the BRD as an ever-existing threat to peace. For this reason, motifs of revanchism, spying and sabotage abounded in most of the fictional works of the DDR during that period, and did not begin to abate until after the construction of the Berlin Wall in 1961. Political relations between East and West Germany did not begin to take on any semblance of normalcy until the election of Willi Brandt as West German Chancellor in 1969.

The psychological impact of the Wall upon the citizens of the DDR was tremendous, and from the point of view of the SED, positive in effect. By halting the flow of political immigration to the West, the Berlin Wall forced many groups, which had formerly resisted integration into the socialist system, to comply with the general trend of consolidation. Justification for the construction of the barrier was not at all a complicated matter. Just as socialist ideology had interpreted the founding of the BRD as a threat intended to impair the peace and safety of German socialism, the same line of reasoning was applied to explain the Wall, not as a means of artifical self-isolation devised to keep the citizens of the DDR within their boundaries, but a device to keep the subversive elements of the West out – a protective device, as it were. The Berlin Wall solidified the process of consolidation in the DDR, led to a greater readiness on the part of the DDR citizens to identify with their state, and manifested a growing self-awareness on the part of the state and the society. Thus, the SED interpretation of history heralds 13 August 1961, the anniversary of the building of the Berlin Wall, as the turning point of inner development in the DDR.

The action of Die Aula (1965), Hermann Kant's first novel, opens approximately one year after the construction of the Wall. Since, as we stated earlier, the literature of the DDR must reflect the culturopolitical development of that nation as it is interpreted by the SED, it is hardly coincidental that Kant proffers a personal interpretation of the historical development of the East German republic that concurs so strongly with the official interpretation. However, he weaves the plot in a manner that ensures that the fate of the individual and the importance of the human condition always emerge as the principle themes of his work.

In the introduction to the international symposium entitled Socialist Humanism, the noted psychoanalyst-philosopher Erich Fromm defines humanism in its simplest terms as the belief in the unity of the human race and in man's potential to perfect himself by his own efforts.[14] Fromm declares in "The Application of Humanist Psychoanalysis to Marx' Theory," his own contribution to the symposium, that:

> Marxism is humanism, and its aim is the full unfolding of man's potentialities; not man as deduced from his ideas of consciousness, but man with his physical and psychic properties, the real man who does not live in a vacuum, but

in a social context, the man who has to produce in order to live.[15]

He points out that Marx stresses the necessity of encouraging and supporting the development of individuality to ensure the greatest possible harmony and universality. Die Aula certainly upholds Fromm's theory. Placing basic human qualities and concerns first, the novel testifies, in my opinion, that Kant, like Fromm, tends to equate Marxist socialism with humanism. Through the medium of his work, the East German author pays warm and sincere tribute to the social progress made by the people of the German Democratic Republic since its founding in 1949. Through Die Aula, Kant reaffirms his belief in the ultimate triumph of the socialist state, which the Marxist ideally interprets as the ultimate triumph of the people.

Essentially an account of the development of sozialistisches Bewusstsein ("socialist consciousness") in a Marxist state, Die Aula examines the personal and political growth of "DDR-Buerger" Robert Iswall, whose path toward socialist maturation parallels the developmental stages undergone by the DDR as a nation. Throughout the novel, Kant points out the strengths, weaknesses, failures, and successes of both the individual and the nation in general. He draws parallels between the development of society and the individual, as it were, and like Walker and Morrison, manipulates situations so that the reader is compelled to acknowledge two facts: (1) that the relationship between individual and society must be mutually fulfilling if it is to yield the most positive results possible; (2) that comprehension of the conditions of the present necessitates understanding the significance of the past. Like the works of the black American feminists, Kant's novel strongly concurs with the Marxist and Hegelian claims that revolution is an evolutionary process, and that it becomes dynamic reality only through the combined efforts of the people. Kant does not envision "the people" as an anonymous group of beings, but as a body of individuals whose distinct talents are amalgamated in order to bring about progressive change for the benefit of society as a whole. Through the depiction of the experience of Robert Iswall, he emphatically calls for the complete development of the individual's character and personality, pointing out on several occasions that identity as a member of the collective, which was a theme stressed in early DDR literary productions, is meaningless, or at best, flawed, unless the personal identity of the individual has been first established. Further, the author demonstrates that it is absolutely inconceivable for any person to achieve the state of genuine socialist consciousness before an honest and positive sense of self-consciousness has been cultivated.

The traditional standards of Western literary criticism would categorize Die Aula, like Meridian and Song of Solomon, as an Erziehungsroman - a novel that investigates the life of a protagonist as he/she attempts to formulate a philosophy of life by learning the nature of the world and the art of living. In writing of Die Aula, East German critic Wolfgang Spiewok maintains, however, that to classify Die Aula merely as a kind of Bildungsroman would be too limiting. From Spiewok's perspective, which is of course, the socialist point of view, Kant's initial novel would be more appropriately classified as a Gesellschaftsroman:

> Die Frage, die sich der Erzaehler stellt ("Wie kann man feststellen, ob die ABF, d.h. Arbeiter- und Bauernfakultaet, der Wissenschaft einen Gewinn gebracht hat?"), impliziert also die Frage nach dem Gewinn, den die gesellschaftshistorischen Veraenderungen der Menschen der Deutschen Demokratischen Republik gebracht haben. Also nicht schlechthin ein Entwicklungsroman, sondern ein Gesellschaftsroman, der in der historischen Bedeutung der Bildungsrevolution die historische Bedeutung sozialistischer Umwaelzungen transparent macht.[16]

For Kant, the mutual relationship between society and the individual has about it a mystical aura similar to the quality that Morrison attributes to the relationship of mother and child; i.e., while maintaining its own sense of self, each entity helps to define or partakes of, to a limited extent, the identity of the other. Die Aula demonstrates that Kant, as a Marxist and a revolutionary artist, recognizes and accepts his moral obligation to inspire and assist the individual identity seeker in the quest for self-knowledge and maturity. In meeting his own social obligation, the revolutionary artist makes it simpler for countless others to fulfill their responsibilities to society. Kant's literary acclaim both in the East and the West can be attributed to the fact that Die Aula was among the first works of literature (if not actually the first) produced in the DDR to present characters who are easily recognized as distinct individuals rather than stereotypic prototypes. Mary Gerber points out that even though it falls chronologically within the Bitterfeld period[17] of East German literature, Kant's first novel differs both in form and content from the industrial novels that generally resulted from the Bitterfeld program.[18] Even the better works produced during that period - De Bruyn's Renata, for example - cannot begin to rival Die Aula for excellence in style or character development. As stated in the preceding chapter, obstacles such as cultural dissimilarities and a variety of others often require revolutionary artists from various national, ethnic, or social backgrounds to respond differently to the requirements of revolution. For this reason, it is somewhat surprising to discover that in many respects, especially from the standpoint of the relationship of individual development to societal development, Die Aula bears a much stronger resemblance to the works of Morrison and Walker than to Renata. While the protagonists of both the East German works are the "positive Helden" required by the standards of socialist realism, Kant's mastery of the dialectical approach allows him to create a hero who remains a positive character even after the flaws in his personality are divulged. In Renata, De Bruyn presents the reader with a picture of a heroine who has already attained a level of socialist consciousness, but because the reader does not know how that character development came about, Renata's behavior cannot be imitated. Kant, however, like the Afro-American authors discussed above, probes the memory and the psyche of his major character, and allows the reader to witness "the development of self-consciousness in the making." His characters emerge as distinct individuals, but they are also the means through which he instructs the audience concerning the importance of distinguishing between a legitimate sense of self and egoism - a lesson vital to any individual who strives for a socialist consciousness.

Although they are not synonymous, humanism and education are closely related. Historically, Western education veritably derives from humanism, and for this reason, it emerges as one of the major themes in Die Aula. The goal of education in the novel, however, extends far beyond the obvious intention of correcting an historical injustice (namely the denial of the worker's right to pursue higher education) perpetrated against one segment of East Germany's society. While it is true that Robert's memoirs describe the education which the candidates of the Arbeiter- und Bauernfakultaet (ABF) received, on a broader or more universal plane, the narrative relates the history of the early years of the DDR, and addresses itself to the task of enlightening an entire nation. Kant obviously concurs with Alice Walker that knowledge and wisdom are the mainstays of revolution. Meridian Hill, the protagonist of Walker's second novel, declares that revolution begins with teaching. The protagonist of Die Aula arrives at the same conclusion, for he observes in a fashion that calls to mind the Socratic method of deduction that, "Ich weiss nur, dass ich fragen muss, wenn ich leben will - so viel habe ich immerhin mitbekommen bei Riebenlamm und Wanda und Haiduck und Danuta...." (p. 300) As Kant's mouthpiece, Robert expresses the author's opinion that life itself is a continuous learning process that must be continually questioned and challenged if it is to have sincere meaning.

To summarize briefly, Die Aula recounts Robert's efforts to compose a suitable, but meaningful, speech to be given at the closing ceremony of the Arbeiter- und Bauernfakultaet (Workers' and Peasants' College).[19] The novel opens in 1962 (one year following the construction of the Berlin Schutzwand ("The Berlin Wall") and the commencement of the second phase of DDR historic development). Robert receives a telegram from Jochen Meibaum, present director and former dean of the ABF, requesting that he deliver the eulogy at the official ceremony. Presently a successful free-lance journalist, Robert had been one of the first candidates admitted to the institute when it opened in 1949, and emerged as class valedictorian upon completion of his studies in 1952. Kant's hero is the classic example of the down-trodden worker who rises to prominence with the help of the socialist party, and thus becomes the perfect public relations image for the affair Meibaum is planning. In short, the socialist director of an institute founded in order to rectify social

injustices – the lack of equal educational opportunities – having
their roots in capitalism hopes to "capitalize" on the experiences
of a fellow socialist. Meibaum sees Robert as living proof of the
success of the ABF. Immediately after he agrees to Meibaum's
request, the protagonist is assigned to cover the story of the Hamburg floods (an actual historical event), since he, like Kant himself,
is originally from that city. The assignment necessarily entails his
traveling to West Germany and taking a figurative journey back in
time. As his train approaches the Bundesrepublik, some unknown
device signals the commencement of Robert's "geistliche Wande-
rungen in die Vergangenheit, " in search of a topic for his speech.

The earliest of these recollections focus on the "lean years" and
the complications hindering development of the infant socialist
state and of the neophyte socialist. As Wolfgang Spiewok points out,
the task facing Robert the journalist is how to determine whether
"the ABF has made a positive contribution to society. "[20] Thirteen
years after its establishment, the institute has fulfilled its "historic mission, " that is to say   that the educational disparities separating working class youth from the descendants of the established
bourgeois and upper classes have been balanced. Robert himself is
proof of this; however, the question remains whether a genuine social contribution has been made. Kant apparently admonishes that
social progress cannot be measured in terms of individual or personal success. He again points out the existence of a bond between
the individual and society in an ideal socialist state. In short, in
Kant's estimation, the success of a project such as that undertaken
by the ABF must be measured in terms of societal progress, which,
in turn, can be determined only by making an assessment of the accomplishments of society as a whole.

As stated on several occasions, comprehending the present is contingent upon having some familiarity with the past, i.e., one cannot
know how far one has progressed without being aware of the point
from which one started. By constructing Die Aula so that it reads
like a series of recollections, Kant drives home the significance of
this point. Heinrich Mohr writes:

Die Szene Demonstrationszug kann als Paradigma fuer das
poetische Verfahren Kants stehen. Der Prozess des Erinnerns konstituiert seinen Roman. Der Erzaehler ist gleich-
zeitig Mittelpunktfigur des Geschehens; ein freier Journalist und Absolvent des ersten Jahrganges der Arbeiter- und
Bauernfakultaet. Er erhaelt den Auftrag, die Festrede bei
der vorgesehenen feierlichen Schliessung der Fakultaet zu
halten. Dieser Auftrag ist die Klammer des Romans, es
stoesst den Prozess des Erinnerns an und ist sein aeusse-
rer Zielpunkt.[21]

Events of the past are relived in Robert's memory. In fact, the
major portion of the novel is given over to the protagonist's recollections of the three years he spends as a member of the ABF and
of the adventures shared with Gerd Trullesand, Jakob Filter, and
Karl-Heinz "Quasi" Riek, his rommates of that period. Although a
good deal of the novel's action takes place in the realm of memory,
at occasional but vitally important intervals, the narrator returns
to the present. This tendency to fluctuate in time, to drift back and
forth from past to present, as it were, creates two separate tem-
poral planes that make it possible for the reader to evaluate the
present on the basis of his analysis of the past. In this manner, the
author forces the reader to experience events of the past vicariously.
He is thus enabled to decide himself whether the ABF has succeeded
in making a positive contribution to the society of the DDR.

The reporting assignment in West Germany is apparently only a
literary device that makes it possible for Kant to achieve two additional ends that are somewhat personal. First, more insight is
given into the protagonist's early life and personal insecurities.
Although Kant adamantly, even vehemently denies that Die Aula is
his autobiography, the novel contains numerous autobiographical
elements. For example, Kant, like the hero of the novel, is a former electrician who fought in the war as a youth and served time
in a prisoner-of-war camp. He also happens to be an Absolvent of
the ABF who has risen to prominence in the literary world. Even
though he denies that Robert's story is his own, only personal experience could have equipped him to construct such vivid murals
of the past. Second, the mission also gives Kant an instrument

through which he airs his personal views about West Germany itself, its citizens, and its relationship to the DDR. While the naked
aggression and open hostility of early DDR literature is noticeably
absent from the novel, Kant projects a subtle negativism toward
the Bundesrepublik. For example, it is certainly no accident that
the difficult and unpleasant memories are recalled at the same
time that Robert is compelled to be in the West. Regardless of
whether the narrator is participating in the present or recalling
the past, a certain tension, which persists throughout the duration
of his stay in Hamburg, can be detected. Finally, in the depiction
of Robert's brother-in-law, Hermann Grieper, "der Gangster,"
Kant portrays West Germany as a land where the rule of criminals
and racketeers prevails, regardless of the wishes of the law-abid-
ing majority. When he departs upon completion of his assignment,
Robert gives the impression that the Bundesrepublik is a land he
would prefer to avoid.

Kant depicts the youthful Robert Iswall as an intelligent, personable
young man with the promise of a bright, positive future despite his
shortcomings. However, like the protagonists of all the works discussed in this dissertation, Robert is an individual alienated by
certain psychological afflictions. The alienation he experiences
has its roots in a deep-seated sense of insecurity directly connected with the war and his personal war experiences. Kant represents Robert as the personification of the DDR itself since most
of the personal problems he encounters are reflections of the difficulties that afflict the state on a nation-wide scale. Kant does not
elaborate upon the horrors of war; however, he does seem to attach some significance to the fact that Robert, who appears to be
the most insecure of the four inhabitants of "Zimmer Roter Oktober," is the eldest and the only one who actually participated in the
war. In addition, the author implies that the loss of his father,
another war victim, has such an unsettling effect upon him, that it
indirectly affects all of his intimate, interpersonal relationships.
In an effort to compensate for what he believes to be his inadequacies, Robert takes refuge behind a sardonic facade, which ultimately earns him the title of Affe Iswall ("Iswall the Ape"). Theodor
Langenbruch suggests that this rather negative appellation alludes

132

to Robert's personal and political immaturity. He refers to Marx
and Nietzsche to support his theory, recalling that the former
speaks of the "Menschwerdung des Affen" when making reference
to the humanization of the "Unmensch," who has been dehumanized
by being the object or subject of economic exploitation. In the case
of Nietzsche, Langenbruch refers the reader to the prologue of
Also Sprach Zarathustra wherein "the brutish ape" is unfavorably
compared to the truly developed human being.[22] In the case of both
Marx and Nietzsche, the underdeveloped character is portrayed in
a negative light, just as Kant takes a dim view of Robert when his
"Affigkeit" becomes overbearing. Like Marx and Nietzsche, however, Kant makes it very clear that he believes in man's ultimate
potential to refine all of his coarseness; i.e., he believes in man's
ability to evolve.

The image Kant presents of the fledgling DDR is not unlike that of
Robert, since both the man and the nation are viewed as inexperi-
enced young entities about to embark upon the path of the unknown.
The author seems to project the opinion, however, that handicaps
withstanding, the DDR and its citizens survive the turbulent years
because they are inspired by a sense of historical justice, belief
in the future, and a special belief in the ability and fellowship of
man. This point is brought home strongly in Robert's rather
lengthy speech, wherein he chides his first girlfriend, Inga, for
her fanatical rejection of the newly founded DDR:

> ... du siehst das alles mit ich weiss nicht wessen Augen.
> Nimm doch mal deine Augen, was hast du denn in deinen
> zwanzig Jahren von diesem Deutschland gesehen als Kano-
> nen und Hakenkreuze und Wehrmachtsberichte und Staedte,
> in denen die Daecher brannten, aber ich will was anderes
> davon sehen. Ich bin durch Polen gezogen und durch ein
> Stueck von Russland, und statt Landschaften habe ich
> Schlachtfelder gesehen, statt zu wandern, bin ich mar-
> schiert, und am Stahlhelmrand war der Himmel zu Ende.
> Das war viellicht eine Empfehlung, wenn du da hinkamst,
> und du warst Deutscher. Ich will aber, dass es eine Em-
> pfehlung wird; ich will nicht mehr, dass die Menschen in
> die Erde kriechen, weil ich komme, und ich will auch

selbst nicht mehr in die Erde hinein muessen, nicht als Sol-
dat und nicht als Gefangener und nicht in einem anderen Land
und nicht zu Hause. Warum siehst du nicht, dass es jetzt
anders sein kann? Wir heissen nicht mehr Deutsches Reich,
wir heissen Deutsche Demokratische Republik, und vielleicht
spuerst du den Unterschied nicht so sehr, du bist vorige
Woche aus einem elenden Dorf zur Schule in die Stadt gefah-
ren, und morgen wirst du wieder aus diesem elenden Dorf
zur Schule in die Stadt fahren, aber ich, ich habe gestern,
als es hiess, wir sind jetzt eine Republik, eine deutsche und
eine demokratische, an diesem Tag habe ich in einem Haus
gewohnt, gerade seit vier Tagen, und das Haus hiess Wohn-
heim der Arbeiter- und Bauern-Fakultaet, and das is ein
Name, der sich genauso selbst zu beissen scheint wie
Deutsche Demokratische Republik, aber das wird sich
fortan nicht mehr beissen, das stimmt von nun an, das
geht jetzt, du, und dir kann ich es ja sagen: Ich konnte vor
Stolz darueber platzen. (pp. 73-74)

Where newly-established nations are concerned, domestic discord
and disharmony often prove to have results more detrimental than
those which stem from the harassment of foreign nations. Prior to
the construction of the Berlin Wall, mass emigration of East German
citizens to West Germany threatened to be one of the most
formidable trials the DDR had to endure. Had it not been halted,
the mass exodus would have undoubtedly crippled the East German
economy. David Childs calculates that eapproximately 2.7 million
refugees fled the DDR between the period spanning 1948 through
1960.[23] This is phenomenal for a nation of roughly seventeen million inhabitants.[24]

In his speech to Inga, Robert casts in his lot entirely with that of
the DDR. When the question of Republiksflucht arises and Robert
is implicated, it is through no fault of his own. Once it becomes
known that his younger sister, Lida, has crossed the border to re-
locate in Hamburg, Robert himself is forced to suffer the consequences of her actions. He is summoned before the directorship of
the ABF, where he is gruellingly interrogated and intimidated.
Only the intercession of the Gruppenleiter, Riebenlamm, and Ro-

bert's best friend, Gerd Trullesand, prevent his expulsion from the institution. As the novel progresses, three other individuals connected with the hero defect to the West: Robert's mother, who flees harassment and unjust imprisonment; fellow ABF candidate Fiebach, who seeks to escape the political haranguing of the reactionary professor, Angelhoff; and finally, Quasi Riek, one of Robert's roommates, whose reasons for defecting are never clearly stated. The defectors are never condemned by the author. In fact, his treatment of them is very sympathetic. At the same time, however, Kant seems to place very strong emphasis upon the determination of the protagonist to remain in the DDR, loyal to his state, despite the "loss" of loved ones, or the persecution of dogmatic political figures.

Since the abolition of alienation is foremost among the goals of socialism, the discussion of alienation, as it exists in socialist nations, is indeed, as Theodor Langenbruch is quick to point out, a very sensitive issue.[25] As mentioned earlier in this chapter, the depiction of the alienated Robert is novel and daring, because it is one of the earliest attempts to represent in a positive light that which Alexander Abusch names "der absonderliche Held." By portraying the protagonist of Die Aula as a man who obviously has some negative character traits, Kant challenges the opinion of a number of noted socialist literary critics. For example, the above-mentioned Abusch writes the following:

> Ich moechte nur auf das Problem aufmerksam machen, dass die Position eines zu "absonderlichen" Helden - als eines im urspruenglichen Sinne des Wortes sich absondernden - die kuenstlerisch-ideele Moeglichkeit zur umfassenden Gestaltung der Entwicklungsfragen unserer sozialistischen Gesellschaft ausserordentlich einengt.[26]

Klaus Jarmatz, critic and editor of Kritik in der Zeit, has similar convictions concerning the figure of the protagonist who is represented as anything other than the "positiver Held" of orthodox socialist realism. Jarmatz expresses his opinion thus:

> Vielmehr kommt alles darauf an, unter welchem Gesichtswinkel so eine Gestalt angelegt ist, ob als queltiger Aus-

druck des sozialistischen Menschenbildes oder als Figur, die in die kritische Distanz gesetzt ist. Als Ausdruck fuer das sozialistische Menschenbild gibt diese Konstellation nichts her.[27]

Both Abusch and Jarmatz are adamant in the demand that the socialist hero be presented as a totally positive figure. Such presentations tend to damage the verisimilitude of a literary work, since the human protagonist must necessarily take on the characteristics of a demi-god. I believe Kant's interpretation of the demands of socialist realism are far more realistic and therefore more meaningful than those demanded by the critics. For Jarmatz and Absuch, the "absonderlicher Held" is a negative figure, capable of giving negative example only. The so-called "positive hero" they require must necessarily be a stock character rather than a developing personality. Kant's outlook is not so narrow. One particular episode expresses the author's rejection of the interpretation of socialist realism as it was determined at the Bitterfeld Conference. As he edits a novella authored by one of the participants of the Bitterfeld Program, Robert sharply criticizes the uniformity and lifelessness of the characters:

> Frau Tuschmanns Novelle kam nicht sehr gut weg in Roberts Besprechung. ... Robert hatte sich vor allem ueber die polierten Charactere in der Geschichte geaergert; sie waren so ebenmaessig wie Billardkugeln und rollten genau dahin, wo Frau Tuschmann sie haben wollte. Dazu gehoerte natuerlich auch schon etwas, und Robert gab durchaus zu, dass die Autorin mit dem Queue umzugehen wusste und sich auf Effet und Winkelberechnung an der Bande verstand, aber es war eben Billard, angewandte Mathematik, und es klappte nur, weil die Kugeln glatt waren und auf einer samtbezogenen Flaeche rollten. Mathematik war eine grossartige Sache; man konnte erwiesenermassen Wichtigeres damit berechnen als Luzifer in Armlaengen und den Standort der Hoelle, sie war nuetzlich beim Billard und bei anderen Dingen, aber eine Geschichte schreiben konnte man damit auf keinen Fall, denn die hatte es mit dem Leben, und das hatte Buckel and Risse, und die Menschen hatten sie auch. (p. 25)

Ironically enough, Kant believes exactly that which Abusch writes, namely that, "Der Held ist also - das zeigt hundertfaeltig die Praxis der Weltliteratur - also ein besonderer Mensch. "[28] Kant implies in Die Aula that variety and diversity can be very positive features in literary characterization. The "negative hero" need not be branded as a totally negative being because his behavior depicts a less-than-positive example in a single instance. While most East German critics, like the two mentioned above, might call for the traditional, inflexible rendition of the positive hero prescribed by the tenets of socialist realism, authors like Kant come much closer to depicting the socialist ideal by portraying in their works the "ewiges Werden" demanded by Marxist ideology.

Much to his credit, Kant does not detract from the significance of the progressive accomplishments of the East German people by attempting to portray the DDR as the classless society of the socialist ideal. On the contrary, he shows keen interest in the relationship between the members of the old established middle class and their newly-promoted counterparts. Mohr calls attention to this: "Ein im Gegenwartsroman der DDR oft aufgegriffenes und vielfach variiertes Thema ist das Verhaeltnis der Neuen Klasse zu den establierten Buergern, das Problem einer Uebergangszeit. " Die Aula concerns itself with the enlightenment of every segment of the society of the German Democratic Republic. However, because their lifestyles undergo the most drastic alterations, Kant seems to focus more closely upon the transition of the members of the former working class.

The great auditorium to which the title of the novel refers is itself a symbol of established, middle-class tradition. The description of its effects upon Robert and Gerd Trullesand, when they first enter it, conveys the idea that the two workers feel their presence in the hall to be a profanation of hallowed ground. The sensation of "foreignness" is in no way diminished by the attitudes the professors and students of the regular university display toward the workers. In fact, their behavior seems designed to imply that the presence of the ABF candidates is a poor joke which must be tolerated. Kant offers two examples which convey the sense of alienation Robert and his comrades must have felt. The first takes the form of a welcome speech from the president of the university, which the ABF students do not understand. At the conclusion of the long-winded, ivory-tower address, the students are left feeling bewildered and more isolated than ever. The election of the student council is the second noticeable event at which a deliberate attempt is made to segregate and ridicule the workers. It is quite a paradox, however, that with the assistance of Hella Schmoeder, a friendly medical student from the bourgeois group, that Quasi Riek is able to reverse the prank and win representation for the students of the ABF.

Not all established academicians are judged in the same light by Kant. Professor Voelshow, to whom Robert and his roommates refer as "Der Alte Fritz," is the exact opposite of the president. He serves as the head of the ABF and constantly urges his charges to "storm the citadel of knowledge." With a poem that calls to mind the Black Nationalist chant of the 1960's, "Power to the People," Voelschow charges his students to challenge the old traditions and forge ahead into the future:

> Wir sind nicht reif / Das ist das Lied, das sie gesungen haben / jahrhundertelang uns armen Waisenknaben," ... "Des Geistes Licht, des Wissens Macht, dem ganzen Wolke sei's gegeben! (p. 49)

Mohr observes that Kant views the problem of clashing social traditions from the perspective of the "Aufsteigenden," the underdogs, as it were. This statement is only partially true. While most of his attention is given over to the plight of the workers, the author in no way implies that the less privileged group is without its own prejudices and intolerance. This is evidenced in Robert's rather shameful behavior toward Hella Schmoeder, whose manners and refinement he strongly resents. He explains his antagonism by claiming that she reminds him of his former girlfriend, Inga, who was also a bastion of bourgeois values. The outrageous behavior of representatives from both groups earns Kant's staunch disapproval. Social stratification is a danger both Morrison and Walker, and the author of Die Aula, are very much aware of. Morrison relates her

138

feelings toward this problem in Song of Solomon, where the bourgeois values of Macon Dead II lead him to absolve all ties with the
less prosperous segment of his family. The aspiration for middle-
class standing results in the death of Macon's niece, Hagar, and
the obliteration of the life-long friendship of the novel's hero,
Milkman Dead, and Guitar Baines. In Walker's Meridian, Anne-
Marion Coles discards her friendship for Meridian Hill once the
relationship becomes bothersome and embarrassing. It would
appear that Kant and the feminists associate social stratification
with pain and destruction. Through his depiction of events in Die
Aula, Kant shows that far more than a new negime and a new name
are required to unite a nation comprised of people who accept social bigotry as a centuries-old tradition. The effort to imbue a
nation with the spirit of socialist equality does not come automatically with the issuance of a governmental decree. Such an effort
must emanate from the hearts of the people.

The socialist claim that the "state and the people are one and the
same" makes the portrayal of the regime of the DDR a very interesting aspect of Die Aula. If we accept Kant's suggestion that there
is a definite parallel between the development and maturation of the
protagonist and that of the state, we must give further consideration
to that particular facet of the novel. The most obvious representatives of the regime - the Socialist Party - are the ABF staff members: Voelschow, Meibaum, Riebenlamm, and Angelhoff. In addition, there is Party Secretary Haiduck, a veteran member of the
Communist Party who participated in the Spanish Civil War. While
he is the only representative of socialist authority who is not an
academician by trade, Haiduck's genuine interest in the ABF candidates and his commitment to the socialist cause make him far
more adept at teaching than the professional educators (with the
possible exception of Professor Riebenlamm). The interaction of
these men with the student members of the ABF represents Kant's
interpretation of the outlook toward education of the East German
Socialist Party during the formative years of the DDR.

Dogmatism, fanaticism, intolerance, and groundless suspicion
are the "vices" of the party representatives to which the author is

most vigorously opposed. These negative traits are depicted in the behavior of Dr. Voelschow, Dean Meibaum, and Professor Angelhoff, three men professing loyalty to a creed which, according to Kant, they don't fully understand. The least objectionable of the three is ABF director Voelschow, a benevolent despot whose redeeming factor is a genuine interest in the welfare of his students. Despite his apparent concern, Voelschow is a rather limited administrator whose inflexible orthodoxy leaves a very narrow margin for individual development or human imperfection. For example it is Voelschow who encourages the ABF students to challenge and overcome every obstacle, to refute the taunting bourgeois class which names the workers the "arme Waisenknaben," by storming the fortress of middle-class tradition, the university. And yet it is the very same man who attempts to dismiss an exceptionally loyal and qualified student from the program, because the youth contracts a mild case of tuberculosis. Ironically enough, the student (Quasi Riek) happens to be a Waisenknabe ("orphan boy") in actuality.

The most negative of the unfavorable models is the fanatical, reactionary Latin instructor, Angelhoff. The over-zealousness of this character often evolves into ruthlessness, and prompts him to commit questionable actions. He joins with Voelschow in the attempt to dismiss Quasi Riek from the ABF. He also accuses Quasi's doctor of subterfuge, and ultimately harasses an inquisitive student until the young man feels forced to flee to West Germany. The equivalent of Morrison's Guitar Baines and Walker's Anne-Marion Coles, Angelhoff is the dangerous internal element that threatens to poison domestic harmony. He is the medium through which Kant strikes out at the harsh, inflexible brand of socialism practiced until after the death of Joseph Stalin in March 1953. (We should remember that the novel was written a few years after Soviet premier Nikita Kruschev had effected de-Stalinization.) The author, it seems, seriously questions the motives of the individual who pledges his energy to the cause of the betterment of mankind, and yet refuses to regard the humanity of his fellow man.

Voelschow and Angelhoff earn the author's disapproval, but Kant actually despises Jochen Meibaum. Of the three negative characters he depicts, Meibaum alone is still active with the ABF in 1962. A perfect example of der Radfahrer ("brown-noser"), Meibaum always does what is proper, regardless of whether it is right or wrong! He is the individual without a sense of integrity, who is not above groveling to ingratiate himself with the powers that be. Meibaum, in short, is a survivor who ensures his survival by any means. He cautions the journalist Iswall that literature, including the ABF closing speech, should present only the positive, i.e., the pleasant aspects of DDR history:

> Ich weiss nicht, Genosse Iswall, ich glaube, deine Auffassung ist nicht voellig richtig; die neue Literatur, die muss doch optimistisch sein, das ergibt sich doch aus unserer neuen Gesellschaftsordnung; das ist, moechte ich sagen, gesetzmaessig. (p. 183)

Predictably, when he suspects that Robert will refuse to comply with his wishes, the event is simply cancelled.

Before judging the regime too hastily, one should consider the position of the DDR in its infant stages. The Stalin era was one wherein the strictest discipline and most absolute party loyalty were demanded. Although Kant approaches the situation with some humor, it cannot be debated that the "Uranfangszeit" of the DDR was indeed a critical and perilous time for the nation, when threats of espionage and sabotage were very much reality. The founders of the DDR felt their position to be precarious insofar as international politics was concerned. The hostility (not imaginary in the least) of the so-called "Free World" was felt very deeply and evoked a great deal of bitterness and suspicion. The actions of Voelschow, Angelhoff, and Meibaum are the results of that demented suspicion.

Interestingly enough, Riebenlamm and Haiduck, the positive authority figures in the novel, actually appear in only two episodes. However, the force of their personalities and the wisdom of their words pervade the entire novel. Not only do they profess the ideology of socialism, but they live according to the creed they verbally embrace. The respect and trust of their subordinates are inspired by honesty, dedication, and good example, as opposed to the empty rhetoric and reactionary theorizing of other characters meant to serve as representatives of authority.

A professor of history, Riebenlamm recognizes education as a form of art, and in his role of "revolutionary artist," stands directly opposed to the pedantics, Angelhoff and Voelschow. It is also Riebenlamm who first recognizes Robert's scholastic potential and urges him to develop it. Riebenlamm is a "professor" in the true sense of the word, impressing upon his students the importance of analyzing the history of man, i.e., searching out the meaning of life through the study of the actions of men down through the ages. In the figure of Riebenlamm, Kant sees encompassed all the qualities the truly proficient and devoted educator should have.

In Secretary Haiduck, Kant envisions the "proper revolutionary." A veteran member of the Communist Party and a former freedom fighter in the Spanish Civil War, Haiduck has long practiced the ideals of socialism and stands in direct opposition to the theorists and reactionaries represented by Voelschow and Meibaum. He is an official of the people who relates and works in close conjunction with the people, as demonstrated in his interactions with the ABF students. Paradoxically, Haiduck, an officer of the Party, criticizes that body more rigorously than anyone else in the novel. He admonishes that reactionary pursuits can cause the individual to lose sight of all that revolution genuinely entails. As evidence, he recalls how the ABF students, in their reactionary zeal, desert one of their fellows. This incident was the campaign of the student "revolutionaries" to have the name of a town square changed from Pommernplatz to Platz der Befreiung. While caught up in the excitement of the demonstration, the students neglect to give proper consideration to Angelhoff's relentless hounding of Fiebach, who ultimately takes the only course he feels left open to him. Haiduck takes the "revolutionaries," especially Robert, to task for what he considers their gross neglect. The most important counsel he offers them is the advice to differentiate carefully between vigilance and mistrust. He voices Kant's own conviction that vigilance is necessary, but fanatical suspicsion is a danger that often results in the alienation of blameless victims. In Haiduck's own words:

> Liebe Genossen, Misstrauen vergiftet die Atmosphaere, Wachsamkeit reinigt sie. Ein wachsamer beobachtet genau, rechnet scharf, denkt, denkt, denkt, fragt immer nach den moeglichen Folgen seiner Schritte aber er geht manchmal rueckwarts, manchmal seitwarts, aber im ganzen immer vorwaerts. Wachsamkeit hat mit Mut zu tun. Misstrauen hat mit Angst zu tun. Misstrauen schiesst auf Gespenster. Das ist Munitionsvergeudung, und die ist strafbar. (p. 113)

Mary Gerber comments that Kant's criticism of the Communist Party is a topic that has been neglected - or simply ignored - by critics from West and East Germany alike.[30] She therefore proceeds to apply her own talents to this undertaking. However, in attempting to prove her point, she gives only marginal attention to the positive elements of the Party. The figure of Secretary Haiduck is barely mentioned and Professor Riebenlamm is ignored altogether. Gerber calls attention to the fact that Haiduck is demoted, because he, i-ronically enough, is the victim of the very fanatical suspicion and false accusations against which he counsels the students. She goes on to imply that the more negative representatives of the Party go unchallenged and unscathed. This implication is totally false. During the course of the novel, Robert encounters Professor Riebenlamm and his former roommate, Jakob Filter, both of whom pass on some interesting information. While it is true that Haiduck is demoted from the level of Party Secretary, he resiliently regroups to advance in other areas. To paraphrase his own words, he moves backwards or sideways in order to progress. As further proof that he believes in the justice of the Party, Kant divulges that Riebenlamm himself, along with many other ABF associates, has advanced over the years. On the other hand, however, all has not fared well with Voelschow, Angelhoff, and Meibaum, as Gerber would have us be-lieve. Like all limited implements, Voelschow is eventually placed on the shelf, as it were. Angelhoff, the disrupter of domestic har-mony is ultimately stricken from the role of Party membership. (p. 294) Meibaum, as stated above, is the only survivor, and there is no doubt that he too will eventually fade away, or be purged from the Party. Gerber, I believe, has overlooked the very point Kant attempts to emphasize, namely, that no one person or select group is the embodiment of the Party. As individuals evolve, then so must the Party evolve, for it is of these individuals that the Party itself is composed.

In Die Aula, Kant has vested Robert and the DDR with the positive potential for development, although the protagonist's actions might often suggest otherwise. Robert, as we established earlier, inclines toward aggressive sarcasm whenever some stimulus - real or imagined - triggers the insecurity that lies latent in his subconscious. If the affliction of insecurity, actually a form of alienation, is, for the most part, attributable to the loss of his father, as I believe, then the defection of Robert's mother and sister to West Germany, coupled with the failure of his relationship with Inga, must have aggravated his psychological imbalance to a very great extent. It would appear that fear of rejection lies at the root of Robert's problems. In all probability, he subconsciously associates death and defection with desertion and/or rejection, and consequently, hesitates to become involved in any situation wherein he would run the risk of incurring the pain of rejection. His closest associates are his roommates, and of those three, only Gerd Trullesand can be called an intimate friend.

While Robert's associates, Trullesand especially, have surmised what it is that plagues their comrade, he himself is quite adept at suppressing the truth. His commitment to socialism and to the cause of the DDR has given him a sense of purpose; as Kant repeatedly implies, identity as a member of the collective is meaningless without a sense of individualism. The refusal to confront himself is a form of self-rejection, which, as we established in the opening pages of this dissertation, is one of the greatest deterrents to positive identity formation. Robert is able to function in a relatively normal fashion until he develops a romantic interest in Vera Bilfert, his future wife. This involvement ultimately leads to the betrayal of Trullesand at Robert's hands. As stated above, affairs of the heart are difficult matters for Robert in any case; however, his feelings for Vera are further complicated, because Trullesand is also interested in her. At the close of their term of study at the

ABF, Robert uses – or abuses – his position as a Party functionary to betray his best friend (Trullesand is married off to another girl and sent to China on a seven-year scholarship to study sinology) and to rid himself of a rival.

Kant offers this episode as proof of his claim concerning collective and individual identity. The Party member whose personal insecurity prompts him to use Party authority to achieve his own ends is far more likely to prove a liability rather than an asset. A member's value to the Party is dependent upon his recognition of his inherent value as an individual.

Kant differs from Morrison and Walker in race, sex, nationality, and ethnic background; yet all three authors make similar statements concerning the effects of psychological battering upon the psyche of the oppressed individual. It is really an irrelevant issue as to whether the individual has been subjected to physical, economic, or any other type of bondage or oppression. When man denies or infringes upon the basic humanity of his fellow man, the negative consequences are far reaching. In my opinion, Kant's depiction of the inhabitants of "Zimmer Roter Oktober" and his selection of Robert Iswall as the protagonist of the novel is very significant. Gerd, Quasi, and Jakob (Robert's roommates) are not so far-fetched that they are unbelievable as characters, but somehow there is still an aura of the hero of orthodox socialist realism about them. They are likeable and sincere. However, each of them lacks any trace of the necessary "hamartia" that enables the reader to identify with him. Trullesand, for example, sacrifices seven years of his life and the right to select his own bride at the behest of the Party. One suspects that Quasi Riek, the Republiksfluechtling, is not a defector in actuality, but an espionage agent for the DDR. By agreeing to exile in West Germany, Quasi foregoes the security and comforts of home and the love of a very devoted woman. Finally, there is Jakob Filter, "der Waldarbeiter ohne Fantasie," whom one would be tempted to name the all around likeable Kumpel ("buddy"). All three characters, despite their winning ways, call to mind Robert's statement concerning the figures in Frau Tuschmann's novella: they are like billiard balls that roll directly where they are cued. However, in this case, Kant implies that they are the instruments of the Party. By painting Robert as an individual with very definite flaws and taints of character, Kant achieves two very effective ends: (1) he provides the reader with an example who is inspirational simply because the reader can identify with him; (2) he places another vote of confidence in the achievements and security of the DDR, for he implies that only those who are firm and secure in themselves have no fear of acknowledging their mistakes or submitting themselves to challenge or constructive criticism.

Notes

[1]Kurt Sontheimer and Wilhelm Bleek, The Government and Politics of East Germany (London: Hutchinson, 1975), p. 16.

[2]Kurt F. Reinhardt, Germany: 2000 Years (New York: (New York: Frederick Ungar, 1961), II, 675-76.

[3]Peter C. Ludz, "Alienation as a Concept in the Social Sciences," Current Sociology, 21 (1973), 15.

[4]Sontheimer and Bleek, p. 21.

[5]Hutchinson (Cambridge), Divided Germany, p. 16.

[6]Sontheimer and Bleek, p. 12.

[7]David Daiches, Critical Approaches to Literature (Englewood Cliffs, N.J.: Prentice Hall, 1956), p. 364.

[8]Sontheimer and Bleek, p. 41.

[9]Hutchinson, Divided Germany, p. 177.

[10]Sontheimer and Bleek, p. 40.

[11]Sontheimer and Bleek, p. 42.

[12]Hutchinson, p. 173.

[13]Sontheimer and Bleek, p. 36.

[14]Erich Fromm, ed., Socialist Humanism (Garden City, New York: Anchor Books/Doubleday, 1966), p. vii.

[15]Erich Fromm, The Application of Humanist Psychoanalysis to Marx's Theory, in Socialist Humanism, ed. Erich Fromm (Garden City: Anchor Books/Doubleday, 1966), p. 228.

[16]Wolfgang Spiewok, "Hermann Kant," in Literatur der DDR, ed. Hans Juergen Geerdts (Stuttgart: Alfred Kroener, 1972), p. 419.

[17] In 1959, the SED introduced a new literary policy at the Bitterfeld Conference, which was designed to "bridge the gap between life and art." Workers were encouraged to write about their labors, while professional writers were urged to leave their desks and join the workers in the factories and fields. Unfortunately, the project enjoyed only minimal success.

[18] Mary Gerber, "Confrontations with Reality in Hermann Kant's Die Aula," Monatshefte, 67, No. 2 (1975), 173.

[19] Following the official founding of the DDR in 1949, one of the first steps taken in the area of educational development was the establishment of the ABF, the historical purpose of which was to give youth from working class backgrounds the same opportunity for higher education as their more privileged counterparts. The ABF prepared the student for successful completion of the Abitur, the examination that determines whether or not the German student may be admitted to a state university.

[20] Hermann Kant, Die Aula (Berlin: Rutter & Loening, 1966), p. 17.

[21] Heinrich Mohr, "Gerechtes Erinnern: Untersuchen zu Thema und Struktur von Hermann Kants Roman 'Die Aula' und einige Anmerkungen zu bundesrepublikanischen Rezensionen," Germanischromanische Monatsschrift, 22, 1974, 228.

[22] Theodor Langenbruch, Dialectical Humor in Hermann Kant's Novel, "Die Aula," (Bonn: Bovier Verlag, Hermann Grundmann, 1975), pp. 26-27.

[23] David Childs, East Germany (New York: Praeger, 1969), pp. 43-44.

[24] Kurt Sontheimer and Wilhelm Bleek, The Government and Politics of East Germany (London: Hutchinson, 1975), p. 103.

[25] Langenbruch, Dialectical Humor, p. 27.

[26] Alexander Abusch, "Zu Werken unser neueren erzaehlenden Literatur," in Kritik in der Zeit: der Sozialismus - seine Literatur - ihre Entwicklung (Halle: Mitteldeutscher Verlag, 1970), p. 594.

[27] Klaus Jarmatz, "Kritik in der Zeit," in Kritik in der Zeit: der Sozialismus - seine Literatur - ihre Entwicklung (Halle: Mitteldeutscher Verlag, 1970), p. 77.

[28] Alexander Abusch, p. 592.

[29] Heinrich Mohr, p. 233.

[30] Mary Gerber, p. 174.

Chapter 7

MORALITY AND CONSCIOUSNESS AS PRESENTED IN DE BRUYN'S RENATA AND BURIDANS ESEL

Evolution, revolution, and development are terms relative to the process of growth and maturation, and as such, emerge as motifs of foremost importance in every work examined in this dissertation. Karl Marx interprets the constant endeavor to bring about positive change in the world as a basic principle of socialism itself. In the thirteenth paragraph of the "Theses on Feuerbach," Marx addresses the issue of change with the following words: "The philosophers have only interpreted the world in various ways; the point, however, is to change it."[1] Marx's statement, it would appear, creates a dialectical situation, for while it is quite obvious that sterile philosophies and hollow theories in themselves will never induce effective change, it is equally certain that thoughtless and therefore empty actions will prove to be just as ineffective in achieving this end. However, two facts remain indisputable: (1) that from the Marxist point of view, the socialist has a moral obligation to encourage and support change for the benefit of mankind; (2) that successful societal change can be effected and maintained only by indiviudals who are personally open and receptive to change, i.e., those with some sense of consciousness pertaining to self and society. An Er-zaehlung of love and politics, Renata is a work which calls for the support of the personal moral convictions of the individual.

There are two versions of Renata. The earlier rendition of the narration appeared in Neue Deutsche Literatur, the official publication of the DDR Schriftstellerverband, a little more than one year prior to the construction of the Wall. The revised edition of the story was published in 1966, and is more pertinent to the political outlook in the DDR today. Renata is somewhat unique when compared with other DDR Erzaehlungen, because it is first a love story and then a political narrative, and also because the protagonist is not a citizen of the DDR, but of Poland. Renata's Polish citizenship is strongly symbolic for two reasons: (1) the invasion of Poland was the act of terrorism which plunged Germany and the world into the Second World War, and meant that the German people were forced to decide whether they would stand for or against the forces of fascism; (2) as a non-German who had suffered extreme hardship at the hands of the Hitler forces, Renata's ultimate ability to overcome her understandable aversion to Germans and distinguish between "Deutschen und Faschisten" is exemplary of what East Germans ideally see as the universality, humanity, and progressive drive of socialism. Renata is a saga of truly ill-matched lovers, who find themselves in a situation similar to that of Shakespeare's immortal characters, Romeo and Juliet. There is, however, one significant difference between the situation portrayed by De Bruyn and that depicted by Shakespeare in his tale of the Montagues and Capulets: the relationship of Romeo and Juliet falls victim to the hatred and enmity between their families; that of Renata and Michael is thwarted by Micha's own personal sense of guilt, which actually overpowers his love for Renata. Like the Germans who voted Hitler to power in 1933, Micha makes a conscious decision (both as a child and as an adult) to pursue his course in life, and cannot, therefore, attribute the consequences thereof to the working of fate.

Renata relates the story of the romance of two young people born in the same time, and actually in the same country, but who, for all intents and purposes, hail from two entirely different worlds. The protagonist is a Polish nurse who encounters a West German school teacher on a Krakau-bound train. The two feel a spontaneous and mutual attraction, arrange a rendezvous, and manage to compact an entire courtship within the space of an evening. Unfortunately, tragic memories from the past emerge to overshadow their whirlwind love affair, and each of the lovers finds himself forced to make a decision, the consequences of which will affect the rest of his and her life. Guenter De Bruyn depicts the incidents which have the greatest bearing on their decisions and convincingly persuades the reader that although the events of the past inevitably come home to affect the present and the future, they can be positively and effectively dealt with if the individual is honest enough to explore every aspect of himself, acknowledge the negative and the positive, and proceed to build a future using the knowledge he has gleaned

from the experiences of the past. The same message is conveyed
by Morrison's character, Milkman Dead, and Walker's Meridian.
It is Micha's inability to come to terms with himself that dooms
his relationship with Renata. De Bruyn gives us an indication that
Micha is reluctant to face the truth about himself and the political
stand of his country in the second chapter of the work. As he and
Renata converse for the first time, the reader is struck immediately by the consuming guilt which gnaws at the young teacher's conscience. An attempt to analyze the shame he feels at being a German
– a West Berliner to be precise – in Poland reveals that he is
inclined to attribute his discomfort to a sense of collective guilt
experienced by the German nation for the atrocities perpetrated
against the Polish people by the Third Reich. This in itself does
not suffice as an adequate explanation, since Michael was a child
during the years of Hitler's rampage. As the conversation progresses, he discusses his approach to politics as a teacher, refer-
ring to his objectivity in dealing with the problematic political situation existing between the two Germanies. At this point, De Bruyn
subtly discloses that a significant part of Michael's emotional imbalance lies herein, for when he remarks about his objectivity as a
teacher, an innocent reply from Renata is interpreted as a stinging
rebuff and an indication that he has merely sought to evade the truth:

> "Ich bin Lehrer, falls Sie das meinen," sagte er, nachdem er
> mich forschend angesehen hatte, "und erzaehle den Kindern
> jedes Jahr, wenn es der Lehrplan vorschreibt, von den ehe-
> maligen deutschen Ostgebieten, nicht mit Hass, nicht mit
> Heimweh, ganz objektiv, Zahlen, Daten. Ist das ein Grund
> zur Scham?"
> "Vielleicht ist das, was Sie objektiv nennen, nur die halbe
> Wahrheit?"[2]

This calls into consideration the paradox confronting the East German
when West Germans acknowledge the guilt of the German nation for the crimes of the Third Reich, while simultaneously allowing former Nazis to occupy positions of prominent importance in the
Bonn government. Perceived from this angle, such a situation supports the East German assumption that restorationist tendencies are
highly prevalent in the West. De Bruyn takes another approach to the

West German inclination toward Revanchismus by having Michael mention his mother and the memories of his early childhood home. Micha's mother serves as a double symbol in the Erzaehlung: (1) by holding on to the memory of Breslau as "die alte Heimat," she is reminiscent of the advocates of the Heim ins Reich Movement of the Nazi era; (2) portrayed as an emotionally and physically broken old woman who continually clings to the past, she is symbolic of the humanistically regressive traits of fascism and provides striking contrast to the progressive nature of socialism:

> "Es war eine traurige Zeit," sagte meine Mutter, als ich spaeter davon erzaehlte, "traurig war alles fort, auch schon vor Vaters Tod. Aber es sollte ja nur ein Uebergang sein, man konnte hoffen. Heute dagegen". ... Und sie weinte wie so oft, wenn von Schlesien die Rede ist. Sie ist sehr alt und einsam.[3]

The ideal socialist, regardless of his/her age, would not experience the same dejection as Frau Schwartz, because the effort to build a new society, in addition to the role attributed to the function of work in a socialist society, would automatically bind the individual to his fellow socialists and give him a purpose in life. On the other hand, the attempt to restore the past amounts to wasted effort.

While discussing childhood memories with Renata. Micha gives the indication that young people in capitalist nations internalize the values of their societies without realizing exactly what is taking place within themselves. Although he claims to be politically objective, Micha makes a comment in the fourth chapter which belies that statement. As Renata speaks about vacations spent in the forests of Wroclaw, he excitedly rejoins that he had been born in that same area, but had few memories of it. The reader marks immediately, however, that the West German insists on calling Wroclaw by its former German name, Breslau, indicating a total disregard for the terms of the Oder-Neisse Treaty, which had returned that region to Polish possession:

> "Sie haben Schulferien bei Breslau verbracht!" sagte er.
> "Und ich bin in Breslau geboren und habe kaum noch Erinne-

rungen daran. Das macht bei uns kein Mensch klar, dass es schon Polen gibt, die Kindheitserinnerungen an Breslau haben. Selbst die einsichtsvollsten Leute glauben, wenigstens gefuehlsmaessig im Recht zu sein. Das muss ich meiner Mutter erzaehlen! "[4]

Although we in the West would be inclined to disregard the West German version of the city's name, the DDR reader, who is aware that West Germans once referred to the DDR as Mitteldeutschland rather than acknowledge the DDR's sovereignty, is more likely to be sensitive to this issue. Political indifference is one of the strongest imputations brought against the citizens of the BRD by those of the DDR. The very tone of Micha's remark is proof of his political ignorance, naivete, or worse chauvinism, since the statement itself indicates that he is not fully aware of the implications of the conditions set down by the Oder-Neisse Treaty, or that he is aware of them, but refuses to accept them.

The tendency of capitalism to alienate the individual is further evidenced by the behavior of Micha himself, as well as that of his mother. Citizens of the West are often portrayed as pleasure seekers by DDR authors. The following statement, however, makes it clear that Micha does not fit wholly into that category:

Ich kam mir so ploetzlich so einsam vor wie auf Festen meiner heiteren Lehrerkollegen.[5]

The sentence above is also an accusation to the effect that even the intelligentsia of the BRD is given over to frivolity and empty socializing. It is possible that De Bruyn is posing the hypothetical question that if those who are responsible for molding young minds have surrendered their positive values in return for the materialist values of capitalism, what hope can there be for the value judgment of those they must educate? Since Micha is not entirely at home in such an atmosphere, De Bruyn is indicating that he is still in the process of developing and trying to find himself, as it were. The author, however, does not take his character to task for searching too long; on the contrary, such an effort is to be applauded if genuine in intent. Micha, rather, falls into the author's disfavor because within himself, he already knows the truth and the answers he is supposedly seeking. Like many other West Germans, for whom he is a prototype, he has become adept at suppressing the truth, because open acknowledgement would be almost tantamount to the loss of material security. Happiness, therefore, is impossible for Micha to achieve until he finds inner peace, or on the other hand, until he casts aside his moral standards tempered by capitalistic materialism. Peter Hutchinson claims that within Micha's personality, there are elements of the "Mitlaeufer," the semi-enthusiastic Nazi, and elements of the "Bundesbuerger," a member of contemporary society who recognizes the moral injustice of restorationist tendencies, but does nothing to stand against them.[6] His ultimate decision with regard to capitalism and socialism strongly influences the fate of his relationship with Renata.

As mentioned earlier, the literary image of the West definitely has some bearing on the group consciousness of the citizens of the DDR. The portrayal of Micha as a likeable, but troubled and confused individual stands in direct opposition to the image portrayed by Renata herself. Unlike the heroes and heroines of many early DDR literary productions, Renata is certainly not a superhuman, self-sacrificing paragon of virtue. As the author points out in the second chapter of the narrative, she is subject to the same desires and vanities as any other young woman her age, and often gives in to them. However, she is exemplary in that she has attained the ability to perceive truth and reality and to deal with her situation according to those perceptions and the dictates of her moral conscience. Whereas Micha is unable or unwilling to come to terms with the entire truth of his past or present life, Renata like Claudia, the protagonist of Morrison's The Bluest Eye, has the ability and determination to do so. That adds to her dimesnion as a well-rounded individual. An example of this is to be found in the scene describing her reaction to the discovery of Micha's nationality:

> Ich dachte nicht: Er ist Auslaender, es wird schwierig
> sein, sich mit ihm zu verstaendigen, er wird bald wieder
> wegfahren. Nein, ich dachte: Er ist Deutscher, und mir fiel
> Papa ein und die Zeit der Besetzung. Es ist nun einmal so,
> dass die Gedankenverbindung zwischen Deutschland und Wehr-
> macht so eng ist wie zwischen Krieg und Tod. Wie das Auge

auf grelles Licht durch Zusammenziehen der Pupille, rea-
giert unser Gedankenmechanismus auf das Wort deutsch
durch Einengung auf Grauuniformierte. Und wie das Auge
erst wieder nach gewisser Zeit sehfaehig wird, koennen
wir dann weiter denken und Unterschiede sehen.[7]

Developing the capacity to deal with her personal feelings proves to
be an important asset for Renata, because it facilitates the process of
interacting with others. Not only does De Bruyn highlight this fact
in the depiction of the protagonist's relationship with the West
German, but also in the scenes portraying her relationships with
her fellow Poles, namely Ruth and her brother, Stefan.

The introduction of Ruth and Stefan is a device employed by the author to re-emphasize what he perceives as the magnanimity of socialism and socialist consciousness. The appearance of Ruth and
Stefan, two Jewish siblings whose parents had perished in Auschwitz,
is a not-so-subtle reminder of the crimes of the Third Reich, ex-
ecuted against the Jewish population of practically the entire conti-
nent of Europe. The fact that Ruth now holds an important position
in a socialist state is an indication that socialism is universal and
abhors bigotry of any kind. This is further evidenced by the fact
that Ruth does not caution Renata about Michael because of any personal hatred she feels for Germans, although one might readily
understand such an antagonistic emotion on her part. The grounds
for her reservations are not based totally upon the experience of the
past; rather, she merely appeals to Renata's sense of reason:

> "Ein Deutscher aus Westberlin, " sagte sie, und ich spürte
> kraenkende Skepsis. "Und was soll daraus werden? Ein klei-
> nes Abenteuer?" ... "Ich wollte dich nicht kraenken, Renia!
> Ich will nur, dass Du wieder zu denken beginnst. Du musst
> dir vorher ueberlegen, was daraus werden soll.[8]

Stefan, who has a romantic interest in Renata himself, does not appeal to her passion, but her reason, urging her to exercise caution.
Though she recognizes the wisdom of what sister and brother say to
her, Renata is bound to act according to her own convictions, which
prove to be sound. She acts, regardless of the consequences, because
she can do nothing else and remain true to herself. However, she is

able to do this only because she is secure within herself and within her role as an individual who has found her niche in the socialist state, of which she is a viable, service-rendering component.

One of the earliest pieces of DDR literature to do so, Renata heralds the advent of the literary trend, which shifted emphasis from the theme of the socialist collective as the primary literary motif to that of the individual and his fortunes as a member of the collective. The earlier rendition of the Erzaehlung, considerably longer than the second edition, stresses political conversion from capitalism to socialism. For example, Micha is surprised to discover how politically conscious the average working man in Poland is as compared to his West German counterpart. De Bruyn presents an episode in which a cab driver gives Micha a political discourse on the difference between the situations in Eastern and Western Europe (specifically West Germany). Naturally, the socialist system is hailed as the more inviting of the two. In addition, much attention is devoted to the condemnation of so-called "Western hypocrisy" and the tendency toward revanchism. When Micha returns to West Berlin, following his encounter with Renata, it is obvious to the reader that the seeds of conversion have been sown in his soul. Ute, his West German girlfriend, tries to discourage the newly forming socialist leanings, warning that the security of his job is more important than the dictates of his conscience. For the first time in his life, Micha recognizes the element of revanchism in his mother's behavior. Frau Schwarz belongs to a group of former Breslauers who hope for the coming of the day when Breslau will again become part of Germany. These people are somewhat reminiscent of the adherents of the Heim ins Reich Bewegung of the Hitler era. Each episode, it seems, is constructed to reassure the socialist reader that he does indeed follow the right path, and to convince the Western reader that capitalism is corrupt and doomed. However, the ultimate decision as to which path to follow is left to the individual. By reaffirming the importance of the individual, his rights, and his intrinsic value as a viable component of his society, De Bruyn hopes to demonstrate that socialism is a means of erradicating the alienation forewarned in Marx's Frühe Schriften.

The personal endeavor of the individual toward change and the concern shown for the success of his ventures are certainly not topics which are new to German literature. In the "Prolog im Himmel," which precedes the opening of Faust, Goethe, perhaps the most versatile of Germany's great visionaries, places in the mouth of the Almighty lines that summarize the ideal attitude of the revolutionary man: "Solang' er auf der Erde lebt, Solange sei dir's nicht verboten. Es irrt der Mensch solang' er strebt."[9] Regardless of whether it is referred to as "das ewige Streben," "das ewige Werden," or "the on-going process of human evolution," man's attempts to improve himself and the human condition will always present a challenge. Still, according to Goethe, Marx, and innumerable other men of vision, the success of human endeavor is inevitable as long as man does not slip into the state of stagnation or complacency. That is, if he is to be successful, the man with a commitment to positive change - the revolutionary - must resist the temptation to cling to any one situation or single moment. For him, as for Faust, to utter the plea, "Verweile doch! Du bist so schoen," would be tantamount to annihilating future development and negating future production. Since socialism demands that each individual contribute to society according to his ability, the socialist would condemn any attempt to stifle social evolution.

The struggle to evolve, "to become" as it were, and the nation's developmental experiences are the themes which have been manifested in the literature of East Germany from 1945 through the present. As stated in chapter six, Die Aula of Hermann Kant applauds the fortitude and determination demonstrated by the East Germans during the formative years of their newly established nation. De Bruyn's Buridans Esel ("Buridan's Ass," 1968) proves to be a fitting sequel to Kant's first novel in that it elaborates upon the themes of growth and maturation, as introduced by Kant. While Buridans Esel is not of the same stylistic significance as Die Aula, the issues it addresses have more relevance for the contemporary East German audience, because De Bruyn concerns himself with the problems encountered in an established rather than a fledgling society. Since the characters of De Bruyn's novel feel the threat of Western interference to a considerably lesser degree than their counter-

parts in Die Aula, the role of the West, per se, does not enjoy any
major importance in Buridans Esel. De Bruyn lets the reader gaze
into the psyche of the characters in such a way as to demonstrate
that even in a so-called progressive society, where humanism is
professed, the individual will emerge as a failure as a human being
if he is not willing to develop a sense of identity and self-consciousness. As stated earlier, the subject of alienation and that of lack of
individual identity, as they exist in socialist societies, can be rather
sensitive issues for obvious reasons. As it relates to these themes
themes, Buridans Esel is a far more controversial work than Die
Aula; however, it ends with the same vote of confidence in the ultimate ability of the truly committed socialist to evolve and refine
himself, and thereby make his proper contribution to society.

Buridans Esel revolves around the triangle involving Karl Erp, his
wife, Elisabeth, and his lover-colleague, Fraeulein Broder (whose
Christian name, incidentally, is never revealed). In itself, the
plot of the novel is fairly simple. Society regards Bibliotheksleiter
Karl Erp as a paragon of success. He heads an important library in
Berlin, is highly respected in his position of worker (white collar
worker though he might be), husband, father, and provider. He
owns a home in the suburb of East Berlin and drives an automobile
that serves as the badge of the success he enjoys. In a general
sense, Erp is comfortably settled in his professional and private
life. Despite all his achievements, however, he feels that some important element, opaque though it might be, is missing from his life,
and he seeks to fill the void through an illicit liaison with Fraeulein
Broder. He pursues the young woman - seventeen years his junior -
to this end, and ultimately wins her confidence. In the course of this
pursuit, he deserts family and home and lives with his lover in a
squalid apartment in the workers' section of the city for a period of
approximately two months. He eventually returns home with the intention of resuming life as though no separation had taken place or
no emotional growth had been achieved. The fact of the matter is
that he alone, of the three major characters involved in the novel,
has profitted nothing from the experience. Viewed from the surface,
it appears that the situation of the Erp household does return to

"normal" once he moves back; however, with the following lines, De Bruyn suggests that things are not really as they appear to be:

> ... mit dem uebrigens das Buch auch haette beginnen koennen: Ein Mann kehrt zu seiner Familie zurueck; die Nachbarn, Freunde, Kollegen, Genossen sagen: Gott sei Dank, endlich, welch Glueck! Und sie halten das fuer einen Sieg der Moral. Der Schreiber aber fragt sich und seine Leser: War es das wirklich?[10]

Morality is a major theme of Buridans Esel. This fact implies nothing out of the ordinary, however, since the tenets of socialist realism uphold "decency" and condemn "decadence." The author intends to analyze the effects that the affair berween Karl Erp and Fraeulein Broder has upon the personal and/or professional lives of all directly affected by it. Along with other so-called "illicit" sexual unions, adultery has been considered and condemned in the works of various DDR authors. For example, Benito Wogatzki criticizes the extramarital affairs of the character, Ursula, in his narrative, Ein Tag und eine Nacht. Werner Braeunig chastisingly points out that Hannes Stuetz, the protagonist of Gewoenliche Leute habitually finds himself in financial difficulty because so much of his salary must be paid out for the support of children conceived in a number of extra-marital affairs. Buridans Esel differs from these works, for while De Bruyn does not condone adultery, neither does he question the morality of it, per se. He concerns himself with the conditions that lead up to the adulterous union, and the actions which result from it. Since it is Karl who takes the initial steps in establishing a relationship with Fraeulein Broder, the reader must determine why he does so.

Understanding Karl's dissatisfaction with his circumstances initially presents us with a problem, since he appears to lead a charmed life. He enjoys the favor of his superiors on a professional level; social approval is his for the asking; and he commands the respect and obedience of his family. In short, Karl can be described as that which Mephistopheles names "der kleine Gott der Welt," albeit in his own private domain. While there is no superficial evidence that might explain his dilemma, the author, through the medium of character analysis, demonstrates that it is actually an acute sense of insecurity that indirectly stimulates Karl's interest in his younger colleague and later drives him to pursue her at all cost.

Karl Erp very obviously suffers from an identity crisis. As stated earlier, his public image enjoys unusually high regard, a fact that is corroborated by Fraeulein Broder's private musings: "Sie hatte sich nach Erp erkundigt. Er war als guter Fachmann bekannt, als Kollege beliebt." (p. 61) However, the constant need to have his self-esteem reinforced through displays of respect, affection and desirability suggest a gross discrepancy between Karl's public image - which includes the facade he displays for the benefit of his immediate family - and the light in which he perceives himself. From the outset, the reader notices that certain tensions are disruptive forces in the Erps' marriage, and while no marriage can be said to be totally free from problems, the union of Karl and Elisabeth is not only imperfect, but decidedly unhealthy. Employing the stream-of-consciousness technique, the author has Elisabeth reveal that the affair with the Broder girl does not mark the first occasion upon which Karl has been unfaithful (pp. 12-13). What appears to be even stranger, at first glance, is the fact that it is Karl himself who makes his wife aware of the extent of his infidelities by stringing off a series of half-truths, i.e., lies, "for her benefit." When one considers the nature of the man, however, the practice does not seem quite so peculiar after all; for by confessing to his wrong-doings and being forgiven, Karl receives further reassurance that he is still the object of Elisabeth's love.

Karl's relationship with his children also gives the reader pause, because it borders on the unnatural. The affiliation De Bruyn describes as existing between parent and child might just as well depict the bond between an owner and his pets. Like Macon Dead II and Mrs. Hill, the elder Erp acknowledges responsiblity for the material well-being of his offspring. He also admits to feeling a certain egotistical pride in the antics of his daughter, which call to mind his ideal perception of himself. For his son, however, Karl Erp can summon no paternal emotions, and openly - even readily - admits to himself that he could easily envision life without either child. In short, the children, like their mother, have meaning for Karl only

160

in that they assist him in defining his role in society and in projecting a certain positive image for the benefit of that same society. As he explains to Elisabeth, he believes, "dass Frau und Kinder und Haus und Garten zu einem gehoeren wie die eigene Hand, das Haar oder die Lippe. ..." (p. 12) Karl's rejection of his children, or the refusal to acknowledge them as distinct individuals also calls to mind Pauline Breedlove, in Morrison's The Bluest Eye. Although the circumstances of his life are drastically different from those that color Pauline's drab existence, Karl suffers from a psychotic syndrome akin to hers, and responds to certain stimuli in a very similar manner. Each character is the victim of a subconscious lack of self-esteem (a fact that becomes more apparent as the story unfolds). This feeling of inferiority manifests itself in the rejection of his/her offspring. The refusal to acknowledge their children is, in effect, a refusal to accept those negative traits they tend to associate with themselves.

A possible additional factor affecting the state of affairs in the Erp household is the very likely suspicion that Karl, despite the success and progress achieved on the professional level, harbors a secret grudge against Elisabeth, because she hails from a class which, by capitalist standards, is economically and socially superior to her husband's. Within the course of the novel, De Bruyn gradually reveals that even the show of material well-being that Karl displays is actually a facade; for the house in the suburbs, the garden and the adjoining land do not comprise communal property, but belong to Elisabeth alone. One of the great ironies of the novel is that Genosse Erp, successful Hauptbibliothekar, is really just an insecure, disgruntled, middle-aged man whose sole possession is an automobile, the symbol of capitalist prosperity. In fact, De Bruyn's "quasi-Held" bears a much stronger resemblance to the traditional image of the West German capitalist, as he is portrayed in DDR literature, as opposed to the idealized hero of socialist realism. By closely scrutinizing all the information and clues the author supplies concerning Karl Erp, the reader is able to conclude that the psychological imbalance and insecurity the protagonist feels are so complicated and so deeply imbedded that only his most intimate acquaintances are able to detect it. For example, since Karl is a man who is obsessed with the idea of putting forth the "proper" public image, only Elisabeth, and perhaps her parents, are aware that he continues to suffer acutely from the stigma of social inferiority - a stigma which exists in his mind only - even after he has achieved considerable social and professional success. As Kant points out in <u>Die Aula</u>, after the official founding of the DDR, the SED took drastic steps to balance social inequalities and correct what were deemed the historical injustices of capitalism by establishing institutions like the <u>Arbeiter- und Bauernfakultaet.</u> Karl, like Robert Iswall, was one of those who profited from those measures:

> Er redet von seiner Laufbahn, von der Schwierigkeiten des Anfangs (der ehemalige Gaertner, Soldat, Kriegsgefangene auf den Baenken der Bibliothekarschule, sie kennt ja Kants <u>Aula,</u> so war es, genauso, schwer und herrlich, herrlich und schwer), von seinen Erfolgen, vom Haus, vom Garten, vom Auto: Alles was man sich ertraeumt hat ist da - und was nun? (pp. 55-56)

At another point in the novel, he reveals that he has never really encountered any obstacles to his career:

> ... Examen, erste Anstellung, Hochzeit, Leerzimmer in der Stadt, Peter, Gehaltserhoehung, Moebel, Radio, eigne Wohnung und so weiter und so weiter. Nichts war ihm missglueckt, in seiner Arbeit hatte er Erfolg gehabt, der anerkannt und honoriert worden war, alle Konflickte hatten sich als loesbar erwiesen, glueckliche Umstaende hatte er zunutze machen koennen, er war gesund, wohlhabend, geachtet, beliebt und mit sich zufrieden.... (p. 16)

Since De Bruyn goes to such great lengths to point out that fortune has been particularly kind to Karl, the reader feels perfectly justified in assuming that the disturbances plaguing the protagonist do not issue from any external source, but from within the man himself. The simple truth of the matter is that Karl has never overcome the feelings of alienation and inferiority which have distressed him since the outset of his career, despite the ample opportunity he has had. He describes those feelings somewhat in a conversation with Kratzsch, a young male colleague:

> Wie hatte er zu Anfang gelitten unter der Grossstadtanonymi-
> taet. War es doch gewohnt, jeden Menschen auf der Strasse
> zu gruessen, von jedem zu wissen, woher er kam, was er
> war, tat und dachte, und daraus folgern zu koennen, wie er
> zu ihm stand. Nur schwer hatte er begreifen koennen, dass
> ihm sein stets waches Interesse an den Nachbarn als auf-
> dringliche Neugier angekreidet wurde, dass man Anteilnahme
> und Hilfsbereitschaft als unerwuenschte Einmischung werte-
> te, ihn ausschloss, isolierte, weil er isolierende Konventio-
> nen nicht achtet. (p. 25)

The sense of inferiority manifests itself in his personal relationships as well. The reader soon deduces that his marriage to Elisabeth was never, from his standpoint, an affair of the heart, but
rather a conquest - a mechanism to bolster his ego. This is veri-
fied by the admission that he exacted a promise from her to stand
by him, "come what may." There is further evidence of his true
feelings in his response to the hypothetical question of why he loves
his wife:

> Und Elisabeth, warum liebte er sie? Weil es ihm wohl war in
> ihrer Naehe, weil er sie staendig ertragen konnte, weil sie
> nie laestig wurde, sich ihm nicht aufdraengte, ihn nicht ein-
> engte, weil sie sich erstaunlich gut auf ihn und seine Arbeit
> eingespielt hatte. Auch Egoismus, also, gewiss, so konnte
> man das nennen, aber wem schadete das, ihr doch wohl
> nicht, nie hatte sie dergleichen zu erkennen gegeben, nie sich
> gegen ihn gewehrt, sie war also doch wohl gluecklich oder
> (vorsichtiger gesagt) zufrieden. (p. 15)

It is rather startling to discover that an individual who places such
a high premium on being loved and appreciated himself fails to respond to or even recognize that same need in others.

Karl is unable to think of his wife without recalling that she has been
a very positive influence where his work is concerned. I believe the
key to deciphering Karl's obsession with the Broder girl and the desperate desire for a relationship with her lies in understanding his
relationship to his work and exactly what work means to him.

Marxism champions the cause of the worker and by virtue of that fact, must therefore have a very high regard for the role of work within society. The Afro-American socialist, Alice Walker, defines work as love made manifest. Anna Seghers, a pioneer and Grande Dame of East German socialism, points out that the dignity and importance of human labor has been represented in the arts for centuries:

> Wir sind nicht die ersten, die menschliche Arbeit darstellen. Schon auf den Stellen des Zeustempels verrichtet Herkules seine Arbeit unter dem Schutz der Goettin Athene. Der arbeitende Mensch ist oft dargestellt worden in grossen Werken der Weltliteratur.[11]

Seghers goes on to indicate that she believes work defines the individual, and that by working in conjunction with others, it helps him to identify (through observing his fellow workers) and define himself:

> Mancher fragt: Glaubst du, dass sich fuer alle das Verhaeltnis zur Arbeit geaendert hat?
> Nein, das glaube ich nicht. Es gibt viele, zu viele Menschen, die noch gar nicht oder kaum verstanden haben, dass sich mit der Gruendung des Staates der Arbeiter und Bauern das Verhaeltnis zur Arbeit geaendert hat. Man kann aber in Arbeitsprozess feststellen - und dann kuenstlerich festhalten - ob sich nichts fuer ihn veraendert hat oder ob ihm alles gleichgueltig ist, ob er langsam, langsam etwas begreift, oder ob er bereits versteht, was da vor sich geht. Sein Charakter wird klar in seinem Verhaeltnis zur Arbeit. An den Besonderheiten der Arbeit erkennt man die Besonderheiten des Charakters. In der Wirklichkeit und in der Darstellung.[12]

Seghers professes that work builds character, but admits in the same breath that many East Germans still have not come to recognize that socialism is responsible for a positive change in the relationship of the worker to his labor. Ironic as it might seem, Karl Erp, Hauptbibliothekar, Chef, honorierter Genosse, etc. is one of those unenlightened unfortunates.

164

In essence, success has spoiled Karl, whose work has, over the years, grown to become no more than a routine function, just like his marriage and home life. Initially, one is at a loss to understand how the successful outcome of projects undertaken for the common good can prove to have adverse effects upon individual character development. However, hidden innuendoes are contained in many of the protagonist's statements. For example, whenever he refers to the success he has enjoyed, Karl always manages to conclude the statement with some reference to his house or car. He makes such a statement the evening he pays his visit - unannounced and uninvited - to Fraeulein Broder: "Er redet von seiner Laufbahn ... von seinen Erfolgen, vom Haus, vom Garten, vom Auto." (p. 55) De Bruyn is emphatic in pointing out time after time that Karl is an individual who thrives on public approval. For example, "Er war als guter Fachmann bekannt, als Kollege beliebt." (p. 61) Or, "Freunde zu haben quaelte ihn. Er war es gewohnt, beliebt zu sein." (p. 29) Or, "Er machte sich beliebt. ..." (p. 154) For Karl Erp, work is neither a form of self-expression nor one of socialist contribution to humanity. Rather, he perceives it as a medium which serves dual functions: (1) it is the means through which he ingratiates himself with those surrounding him in order to be ensured of the receipt of much-needed ego-bolstering and reinforcement of self-esteem; (2) it supplies him with the income to maintain a lifestyle admired by his peers and affords him the "privilege" of ruling family and household despotically if benevolently. Over the years, he settles comfortably into this routine, relieving occasional fits of boredom or melancholy with casual love affairs. Because he has achieved what he wants - acceptance, social standing and financial security - he is no longer inspired to approach his work innovatively or energetically. Even his superiors are aware of this. In an attempt to force him to break off the affair with Fraeulein Broder, one of them makes the same accusation in the form of the following implication:

> Aber Mantek lag nichts an dem Wort, was er meinte war das: Karls Elan hatte mit seiner Jugend geendet, er war muede geworden, hatte sich zur Ruhe gesetzt, jeden Ehrgeiz aufgegeben und sich jetzt noch zu Haus und Auto die Geliebte angeschafft. (p. 166)

The irony of the situation lies in the fact that Karl, who has profited
so much from the socialist interpretation of the social function of
work, and who is an important authority figure, actually lacks Ar-
beitsmoral ("the moral consciousness") which results from working
for the good of the socialist society. It would appear that De Bruyn
is also questioning the suitability of superiors who are aware of this
deficiency and yet allow such an individual to remain in authority.
For our purposes, it is sufficient to realize at this point that Karl
is obsessed with the younger woman because she appeals to him
intellectually as well as physically. Her intellect and composure
stimulate something that has lain dormant within him for years. He
perceives in her the best qualities of his own and Elisabeth's youth.
In fact, he sees her in the same light as he had seen Elisabeth
years ago: she offers him the opportuniy to make another "meaningful conquest," and therefore poses a challenge to his masculinity
and intellect. Since his feelings toward Fraeulein Broder have more
to do with ego than love, it is not surprising to find that after two
months of living under uncomfortable, even squalid conditions at her
home, and facing the wrath of his superiors and public disapproval
at work, Karl is secrety relieved that the affair comes to an end and
that his lover is departing. To paraphrase De Bruyn, he watches
her go "with a bleeding heart -- a bleeding heart from which a weight
has fallen." (p. 237) Fraeulein Broder's departure clears the way
for Karl to return to his family - peace with honor, as it were.
However, De Bruyn assures the reader that on the home front at
least, he will find that "der kleine Gott der Welt" is no more.

As stated earlier, the act of adultery is not the moral issue that interests the author. De Bruyn seems to imply that he can accept, if
not condone, the fact that episodes of infidelity do occur. Although
Karl Erp can offer no excuse for his discrepancies, De Bruyn still
does not take him to task for having had an extra-marital affair. The
author condemns the protagonist's reasons for pursuing the liaison
in the first place, the total disregard he displays for the feelings of
everyone involved, especially his wife and his mistress, and the
refusal to meet his responsibilities. There is no doubt that Karl
bears a close resemblance to the French philosopher's jackass from
which the novel takes its title. Legend has it that the donkey stood

between two bundles of hay, but starved to death because he could not decide which of the to two eat. Karl would like to maintain a relationship with his wife and his lover; but finding himself faced with the same dilemma as his four-legged counterpart, he eventually loses both women. Unfortunately, Karl is not the only one who suffers from his actions, a fact which the author repeatedly points out. De Bruyn presents an Iron Curtain-country authority figure who has at least four Afro-American literary doubles, for Karl, Macon Dead II, Mrs. Hill, and Pauline and Cholly Breedlove are all fashioned from the same mold. Each character, himself a victim of social injustice, seeks to subject others (notably members of his immediate family) to the same or similar ignominies. Despite racial, social, and national differences, a deeply ingrained sense of inferiority drives the above-named characters to find subconscious reinforcement of self-esteem by observing the humiliation of others. Although such remedies may serve to assuage the pain of such a deep-seated affliction, the relief is, of course, only temporary.

Karl has the uncanny ability to turn a deaf ear to anything unpleasant or to rationalize that which he cannot ignore. In presenting Karl Erp, De Bruyn has surpassed Hermann Kant in the depiction of the highly unorthodox "negativer Held." Karl also reminds the reader of Morrison's Macon Dead II, or Walker's Truman Held, in his ability, or better, his willingness to sacrifice the emotional well-being of family members and intimate friends in order to achieve his own designs. In other words, no price is too great to pay for what Karl wants as long as he himself is not called upon to render payment. If we assume that Erich Fromm's equating of socialism with humanism is valid, we can deduce that Karl is a failure as a socialist because he is a failure as a human being. Once he achieves the desired goal of his life - financial security and social approval - he ceases to be productive, ceases to really care about the work which made it possible for him to achieve a modicum of success. Once the desire for material gain has been fulfilled, Karl, of his own accord, halts the process of his personal development. He ceases to strive and therefore ceases to evolve as a human being. The Marxist Anschauung condemns such an action as a "mortal sin," as it were. However, the undisguised attempt to rob Elisabeth of the chance to develop as an individual (by maneuvering her into the traditional bourgeois role of housewife) would surely be classified as a "cardinal sin." By intermittently reminding the reader that Karl enjoys acting out the role of "der Chef" and "paterfamilias," De Bruyn stresses that Karl wields a great deal of influence and authority. Authority has its privileges, but also its responsibilities. A reader who bases judgment upon the tenets of orthodox socialist realism (like the Western reader) would assume that Karl's involvement with building the new society of the DDR should have given him the means to change his attitudes and value system from the middle class perspective to that of socialism. This has not been the case, and yet, this same individual occupies a prominent position within the hierarchy of the Party structure, and has a great amount of influence on an untold number of lives. De Bruyn challenges the morality of the act which sanctions giving power to a man who has proved unworthy of trust and responsibility. That Karl lacks a sense of personal integrity and fails in his responsibility to his family is tragic in itself. De Bruyn, however, finds it inexplicable and totally unacceptable that authority should be once again entrusted to him.

Ideally, Marxist societies view socialism as a new quality in human relationships, which is characterized by friendly cooperation and mutual help.[13] Since the principles of socialist morality proclaim the equality of all people, one of the goals of socialism is the realization of equal opportunity for every individual, using his ability and achievements as guidelines to establish merit. Toni Morrison and Alice Walker both point out that in Western societies, most women, regardless of race, creed, or nationality, have traditionally been the victims of sexual bigotry since time immemorial. With the advance of technology and the increased interest in production, women have come to suffer oppression as workers as well as females. For these reasons, socialist ideals have a very special meaning also for the woman of Marxist nations, because the ideals of socialism seek to guarantee the female the rights and equality traditionally withheld from her in paternalistic societies. Through the portrayal of Elisabeth Erp and Fraeulein Broder, De Bruyn demonstrates that he recognizes the intrinsic worth of the female as an individual and highlights the role of women in the socialist society. Each of the characters is presented from the standpoint of her relationship with Karl, and they are both portrayed in a far more positive and favorable light than he. De Bruyn constructs the novel in this fashion to show the scorn he feels for the paternalistic outlook which conceives of the male as a character who commands admiration and obedience simply by virtue of his gender. He does not condone the absolute authority of the patriarch or the subservience of the female. Obviously, the enlightenment of the parental generation, or at least one segment thereof, is a prerequisite for an enlightened future generation. Since the woman is normally the transmitter of culture and enlightenment, as Morrison and Walker repeatedly point out in their novels, it appears that it would behoove any society - socialist or otherwise - to educate the female in terms of the social values it views with favor. This is one of the messages De Bruyn seeks to convey.

Gleichberechtigung ("equal rights"), Bewusstsein ("consciousness"), and Selbstbewusstsein ("self-consciousness") are ideal characteristics of the socialist society and therefore emerge as prominent themes in Buridans Esel. Elisabeth is the vehicle through which De Bruyn introduces them. Although she emerges as a forceful, developing character in the latter half of the novel, in the first half, she is a lethargic, almost comatose woman whose entire existence is centered in her house and around her family. We are able to glean quite a bit of information about her background and her life, but tend to think of her in terms of being "Karl's wife," because that is exactly how she perceives herself. In fact, she explains to Karl's superior, Theo Hassler, that for years she has thought of herself as her husband's satellite:

> Spaeter wird sie einem Mann (nicht ihrem) das zu erklaeren versuchen, mit dem Bild des Trabanten, der das groessere Gestirn umkreist, umkreisen muss, weil, das (seit Jahren unartikuliert angezweifelte) Gesetz der Liebe es befiehlt, es zu befehlen scheint. (p. 13)

The statement above gives the reader pause, because Elisabeth is a well-educated woman. (Like her husband, she is a trained librarian.) To encounter such an attitude in a fairly young citizen of a Marxist nation is indeed perplexing, until the audience recalls that Elisabeth has grown up as a member of the privileged middle class. Karl points out that the atmosphere of her home had been particularly loving, but nevertheless, one in which the traditional, Western paternalistic value system prevailed. Therefore, in her own marriage, she accepts without protest the norm which consigns her to the realm of the home and gives her husband unlimited freedom of movement. It is, I believe, quite symbolic that the Erps are living in Elisabeth's childhood home, for Karl has always looked upon it as a symbol of his social and economic acceptance into the "in crowd," as it were. The house is meant to depict a symbolic fortress of bourgeois values and beliefs. De Bruyn unhesitatingly acknowledges the fact that Elisabeth suffers as a result of the lifestyle she follows, and that she is decidedly insecure and unhappy:

> Vielleicht glueckte der Versuch (um Beunruhigen und Eifersucht zu unterdruecken) weil Muehe, Schwere, Schmerz genug da waren, so dass Erps Treibhauslieben (die am Abend erbluehen, am morgen abfallen) dagegen leicht scheinen.
> (pp. 12-13)

Elisabeth, by her silent acceptance of Karl's abuses and acquiescence to his chauvinistic demands, reinforces the same system that subjugates her, i.e., she herself contributes to the immorality of human oppression. De Bruyn implies that Elisabeth finds herself in uncomfortable circumstances as a matter of choice rather than force. By playing the role of subservient housewife, Elisabeth demonstrates a certain inclination toward the self-image of the victim or that of the martyr. However, she does not take into account that she is voluntarily allowing her talents to lie fallow. Maximum quality production receives top priority in the socialist society, and therefore, the waste of talent and energy is interpreted as a form of decadence. As stated previously, socialism makes demands upon the individual according to his ability and achievements. In her lethargic state, Elisabeth makes no meaningful contribution to her society, and for that reason, can lay no claim to the sympathy of the author. One of the principal aims of Buridans Esel is to encourage socialist consciousness by stressing the importance of socialist morality. Morality is, of course, contingent upon personal integrity, and therefore, De Bruyn cannot show support for a character who offends integrity for the sake of a charade. Only after she begins to exert herself on her own behalf - when she shows signs of developing a sense of self - does De Bruyn start to champion Elisabeth's cause.

A sense of outraged dignity prompts Elisabeth to face the reality of her situation with Karl and to accept responsibility for her own life and destiny. Through twelve years of marriage, she endures mental castigation at his hands, while clinging desperately to her belief that despite all, her husband loves her. She describes her belittlement in the following manner:

> Die Sache war so: Erp wusste alles besser als sie, tatsaechlich, war er gebildeter, geschulter, beschlagener, erfahrener, hatte mehr gelernt, mehr gesehen, mehr erlebt und gruendlicher nachgedacht. Und er zeigte es ihr taeglich. (p. 83)

When the extent of Karl's affair with Fraeulein Broder is fully exposed and he is forced to openly discuss the matter with Elisabeth, he denies that he has ever loved his wife, stating further that he expects her to be patient with him until he can decide whether he really loves the younger woman. This statement destroys Elisabeth's illusions, and in effect actually frees her, because from that point on, she accepts responsibility for her own life and begins to search for her own place in society. As one might expect, this process involves finding meaningful, suitable employment. With the help of Theo Hassler, she first secures a librarian's position, but eventually moves on to the new profession of art historian. When Karl returns to his family following Fraeulein Broder's departure, he discovers that Elisabeth is no longer a thrall willing to exchange individuality for the promise of love and financial security. Her growing self-consciousness has stimulated the development of socialist consciousness. De Bruyn portrays her as being inclined toward the realization that a profession is not merely a source of income, but a life task. Her profession will put her on the path to becoming reintegrated with society.

David Childs points out that the constitution of East Germany specifically states that women are equal to men under the law.[14] In the report, The German Democratic Republic from the Sixties to the Seventies, political scientist Peter C. Ludz reports a pronounced incorporation of married women into the labor force, a fact that suggests that some attempt is being made to exercise the rights guaranteed by the constitution.[15] De Bruyn's tale of an East German woman's awakening consciousness was undoubtedly influenced by the New Family Law of the DDR, which was put into effect in April 1966. Most of the problematical situations arising between Karl and Elisabeth stem from issues specifically addressed in the new legal code. For example, the law specifies that a husband may not prevent his wife from working, that the household chores should be the responsibility of both marital partners, and that in the event of divorce, the husband is required to pay child support, but not alimony if the wife is physically able to work. Karl mentions that he would not be required to support Elisabeth in the event of divorce, indicating that the law has been put into practice. It is rather typical of Karl that he is willing to adhere to the stipulations of the law that would benefit him, while ignoring those concerned with protecting his wife. The reader can only conclude that the author believes that even the best of laws are without value if those for whom they are written lack morality and/or consciousness.

Just as Elisabeth Erp is the medium through which De Bruyn works to describe the awakening of individual consciousness, Fraeulein Broder provides him the means to depict the developed socialist personality. While traditional moralists, represented by Karl's Spiessbuerger superiors, Fred Mantek and Theo Hassler (who refer to Fraeulein Broder as "der Totengraeber eines Lebensstils," are quick to condemn the young woman for her involvement with a married man, she is actually the most moral of all the characters presented in the novel. In addition, she bears a striking resemblance to her forerunner, Renata, in that both young women have developed a sense of socialist consciousness that allows them to act according to the dictates of their individual conscience, despite conventional rules and public expectations.

172

Although she is the only character in the novel who has actually attained the goal of sozialistisches Bewusstsein, Fraeulein Broder possesses no extraordinary or spectacular characteristics which suggest that she is more or less than an ordinary human being. De Bruyn supplies some information about her family history, but gives no clues concerning the intimate details of her life. Her Christian name is never divulged and we know only that she, like Karl and the protagonist of Die Aula, hails from a working class background. The young woman makes good use of the opportunities offered by socialist reforms to improve her lot in life, so that when she is first introduced into the novel, she emerges as a very self-assured individual whose sense of self and attitude toward her work gives her the air of professionalism that first attracts Karl's attention:

> ... kein Zug ihres Gesichts an Verklemmtheit oder Arroganz. Sie gab sich locker, sicher, selbstbewusst, sprach Hochdeutsch ohne Dialekteinschlag oder Krampf und versuchte nicht zu blenden, nicht zu kokettierren. Dass Erp ihr Chef war und ein Mann, schien keinen Einfluss auf sie zu haben. Sie blieb kuehl und liess kuehl. (p. 9)

She is, in effect, one of the "gewoehnliche Leute" about whom Werner Braeunig writes - a socialist "Jedermann," so to speak. However, De Bruyn does not use her as a person to emulate in the struggle towards socialist consciousness; for although he portrays her as having achieved that desired goal, he never explains how she does it. (This is the same approach he takes in Renata.) It appears, rather, that she is the standard used to highlight Karl's regression and Elisabeth's progress. Fraeulein Broder is not strikingly different from either of the other two central characters. She is neither exceptionally virtuous nor exceptionally passive; i.e., she is subject to the same desires and temptations as any other human being and sometimes submits to them, as her involvement with Karl demonstrates. She does, however, cling to the tenets of her personal integrity, and this means that she refuses to lie to herself. Unlike Karl and Elisabeth, she never has to come to terms with living a lie and elects to follow the dictates of her conscience even though doing so proves to be bitterly painful. At the close of her two months with

Karl, she is forced to make an appraisal of her relationship with him, and although she had not been oblivious to his faults before, she realizes for the first time that life with him would require that she give up her work and her lifestyle to ensure that no sense of rivalry mars their relationship. He, on the other hand, would make no concessions. Fred Mantek's accusation is correct. Karl has become staid and stagnant. Having lost the socialist enthusiasm for his work, he doesn't recognize the importance it has for his lover. For the dedicated socialist, life without work is the equivalent of life-in-death; for it is existence without productivity and meaning. Despite the pain of separation, Fraeulein Broder moves on in search of the outlet that will allow her to fulfill her potentialities, while her former paramour, who profits absolutely nothing from the experience, seeks to climb back into the same stagnant pool from which he had briefly emerged. While there seems to be no hope that Karl will ever change, the novel certainly does not end on a pessimistic note, for in the personalities of Elisabeth and Fraeulein Broder, De Bruyn sums up the Faustian spirit that would challenge hell itself in order to pursue life's goals.

Notes

[1]Karl Marx, "Theses on Feuerbach," in Marx and Engels: Basic Writings on Politics and Philosophy, ed. by Lewis S. Feuer (Garden City, New York: Anchor Books/Doubleday, 1959), p. 245.

[2]Guenter De Bruyn, "Renata," in Fahrt mit der S-Bahn, hrsg. Lutz-W. Wolff (Muenchen: Deutscher Taschenbuch Verlag, 1972), p. 210.

[3]De Bruyn, Renata, p. 205.

[4]De Bruyn, Renata, p. 216.

[5]De Bruyn, Renata, p. 205.

[6]Hutchinson, Divided Germany, p. 155.

[7]De Bruyn, Renata, p. 208.

[8]De Bruyn, Renata, p. 214.

[9]Johann Wolfgang von Goethe, Faust (Munich: C. H. Beck, 1972), p. 18.

[10]Guenter De Bruyn, Buridans Esel (Halle (Saale): Mitteldeutscher Verlag, 1968), p. 245. (All quotations taken from this edition.)

[11]Anna Seghers, "Der Tiefe und Breite in der Literatur," in Kritik in der Zeit: Der Sozialismus - seine Literatur - ihre Entwicklung, ed. by Klaus Jarmatz (Halle (Saale): Mitteldeutscher Verlag, 1970), p. 490.

[12]Anna Seghers, pp. 490-491.

[13]Kurt Sontheimer and Wilhelm Bleek, The Government and Politics of East Germany (London: Hutchinson, 1975), p. 41.

[14]David Childs, East Germany (New York: Praeger, 1969), p. 219.

[15]Peter C. Ludz, The German Democratic Republic from the Sixties to the Seventies: A Socio-Political Analysis (Cambridge, Massachusetss: Center for International Affairs, Harvard University, 1970), p. 23.

CONCLUSION

Since human beings are creatures much given to communal interaction, it is very logical to assume that many of the afflictions plaguing the individual will affect his attempts at social intercourse. While a survey of the history of mankind might suggest that man's inhumanity toward his fellowmen poses the most outstanding impediment to the course of human development, authors such as Walker, De Bruyn, Kant, and Morrison strongly argue that it is the individual's inability to accept or relate to himself that damages his relationships with others, and thus impedes social progress. This dissertation has sought to compare the writing of the above-mentioned novelists in an attempt to prove that alienation has the same damaging effect (some form of ego-obliteration) upon all members of the family of mankind, regardless of the many variances that tend to set one group apart from another. This study also seeks to proffer self-consciousness and self-acceptance as universal remedies for the ailment of ego-defacement.

It is not suggested here that Morrison, Kant, Walker, and De Bruyn are the first to recognize and identify alienation as the most lethal of the social ills. On the contrary, Richard Wright, Arnold Zweig, W. E. B. Du Bois, and Karl Marx himself, among countless others, have addressed that issue over the decades. However, the authors whose works have been examined in this study are revolutionaries in that they rank among the earliest contemprary writers who advocate constructive criticism of a given society, while continuing to work within the parameters of that same society.

While this dissertation is the first thesis to undertake a comparative study of personality development in East German and Afro-American literature, it has in no way exhausted the theme. Rather, this initial exploration has merely scratched the surface of discovery and points the way to further investigation into the personality development of citizens who reside within a nation while simultaneously residing without.

SELECTED BIBLIOGRAPHY

Allen, Robert L. Black Awakening in Capitalist America. Garden City, N.Y.: Anchor Books, 1969.

Baldwin, James. The Fire Next Time. New York: Dial Press, 1963.

Bandler, Michael J. "Novelist Toni Morrison: 'We Bear Witness.'" Africa Woman, Sept.-Oct. 1979, p. 28.

Banks, James A., and Jean D. Grambs, eds. Black Self-Concept. New York: McGraw-Hill, 1972.

Bell, Roseann P., Betty J. Parker, and Beverly Guy-Sheftall, eds. Sturdy Black Bridges. Garden City: Anchor Press/Doubleday, 1979.

Benson, Lou. Images, Heroes, and Self-Perceptions: the Struggle For Identity, From Mask-Wearing to Authenticity. Englewood Cliffs: Prentice-Hall, 1974.

Berghahn, Marion. Images of Africa in Black American Literature. London: Macmillian, 1977.

Billingsley, Andrew. Black Families in White America. Englewood Cliffs: Prentice-Hall, 1968.

Bone, Robert A. The Negro Novel in America. New Haven: Yale University Press, 1965

Bowles, Juliette, ed. In the Memory and Spirit of Frances, Zora, and Lorraine: Essays and Interview on Black Women and Writing. Washington, D.C.: Institute for the Arts and Humanities, Howard University, 1979.

Brown, Sterling. The Negro in American Fiction. Albany: J.B. Lyon, 1937.

Childs, David. East Germany. New York: Praeger, 1969.

Coffin, Tristam Potter. The Female Hero in Folklore and Legend. New York: Pocket Books, 1975.

Cook, Mercer, and Stephen Henderson. The Militant Black Writer. Madison: University of Wisconsin Press, 1969.

Coombs, Norman. The Black Experience in America. New York: Twayne Publishers, 1972.

Crain, Robert L., and Carol S. Weisman. Discrimination, Personality, and Achievement. New York: Seminar Press, 1972.

Daiches, David. Critical Approaches to Literature. Englewood Cliffs, N.J.: Prentice-Hall, 1956.

De Bruyn, Guenter. Buridans Esel. Halle (Saale): Mitteldeutscher Verlag, 1968.

--- "Renata." In Fahrt mit der S-Bahn. Hrsg. Lutz-W. Wolff. Muenchen: Deutscher Taschenbuch Verlag, 1972.

Dorson, Richard M. American Negro Folktales. Greenwich, Conn.: Fawcett Publications, 1956.

Dorling, Colette. "The Song of Toni Morrison." New York Times Magazine, 20 May 1979, p. 58.

Eifler, Margret. Dialektische Dynamik: Kulturpolitik und Aesthetik im Gegenwartsroman der DDR. Bonn: Bovier Verlag, Herbert Grundmann, 1976.

Firestone, Shulamith. The Dialectic of Sex. New York: Bantam Books, 1971.

Frazier, E. Franklin. Black Bourgeoisie: The Rise of a New Middle Class in the United States. New York: Collier Books, 1962.

--- The Negro Family in the United States. New York: Dryden Press, 1948.

Fromm, Erich. "The Application of Humanist Psychoanalysis to Marx's Theory." In Socialist Humanism. Ed. Erich Fromm. Garden City: Anchor Books/Doubleday, 1966.

--- Socialist Humanism. Garden City: Anchor Books/Doubleday, 1966.

Gayle, Addison, Jr., ed. The Black Aesthetic. Garden City: Anchor Books/Doubleday, 1972.

Gayle, Addison, Jr., ed. The Way of the New World: The Black Novel in America. Garden City: Anchor Books, 1976.

Geerdts, Hans Juergen, ed. Literatur der DDR in Einzeldarstellungen. Stuttgart: Alfred Kroener, 1972.

Gerber, Mary. "Confrontations with Reality in Hermann Kant's Die Aula." Monatshefte, 67 (1975), 173-84.

Ginzberg, Eli, and Alfred S. Eichner. The Troublesome Presence. New York: Mentor Books, 1964.

Goethe, Johann Wolfgang v. Faust. Munich: C.H. Beck, 1972.

Greenberg, Harold, ed. Social Environment and Behavior. Cambridge, Mass.: Schenkman Publishing Co., 1971.

Grier, William H., and Price M. Cobbs. Black Rage. New York: Bantam Books, 1969.

Gross, Seymour L., and John E. Hardy, eds. Images of the Negro in American Literature. Chicago: University of Chicago Press, 1966.

Hamburger, Michael, ed. East German Poetry: An Anthology. New York: E.P. Dutton, 1973.

Hanhardt, Arthur, Jr. German Democratic Republic. Baltimore: Johns Hopkins Press, 1968.

Harper, Michael S., and Robert B. Stepto. Chant of Saints. Urbana: University of Illinois Press, 1979.

Harris, Trudier. "Violence in the Third Life of Grange Copeland." College Language Association Journal, 19 (1975), 238-47.

Harris-Schenz, Beverly. "Images of the Black in Eighteenth Century Literature." Diss. Stanford University, 1977.

Heitner, Robert R., ed. The Contemporary Novel in German: A Symposium. Austin: University of Texas Press, 1967.

Hornstein, Lillian, G.D. Percy and Sterling Brown, eds. The Reader's Companion to World Literature. New York: New American Library, 1973.

Huggins, Nathan I. Harlem Renaissance. London: Oxford University Press, 1971.

Hutchinson, Peter. Literary Presentations of Divided Germany: The Development of a Central Theme in East German Fiction 1945-1970. Cambridge: Cambridge University Press, 1977.

Jahn, Janheinz. Neo-African Literature: A History of Black Writing. New York: Grove Press, 1968.

Jarmatz, Klaus. Forschungsfeld Realismus: Theorie, Geschichte, Gegenwart. Berlin: Aufbau-Verlag, 1975.

--- Kritik in der Zeit: Der Sozialismus - seine Literatur - ihre Entwicklung. Halle (Saale): Mitteldeutscher Verlag, 1970.

Jeffers, Trellie. "The Black Black Woman and the Black Middle Class." Black Scholar, March-April 1973, pp. 36-37.

Johnson, Frank, ed. Alienation: Concept, Term, and Meanings. New York: Seminar Press, 1973.

Jordan, Winthrop D. The White Man's Burden: Historical Origins of Racism in the United States. London: Oxford University Press, 1974.

Kant, Hermann. Die Aula. Berlin: Rutten and Loening, 1966.

Kardiner, Abram, and Lionel Ovesey. The Mark of Oppression. Cleveland: World Publishing Company, 1967.

Karenga, Ron. "Black Cultural Nationalism." In The Black Aesthetic. Ed. Addison Gayle, Jr. Garden City: Anchor Books/Doubleday, 1972.

Kearns, Francis E. Black Identity. New York: Holt, Rinehart and Winston, 1970.

Kent, George E. Blackness and the Adventure of Western Culture. Chicago: Third World Press, 1972.

Langenbruch, Theodor. Dialectical Humor in Hermann Kant's Novel "Die Aula." Bonn: Bovier Verlag, Hermann Grundmann, 1975.

Legters, Lyman H. The German Democratic Republic: A Developed Socialist Society. Boulder: Westview Press, 1978.

Lerner, Gerda, ed. Black Women in White America: A Documentary History. New York: Vintage Books, 1973.

Lincoln, C. Eric. The Negro Pilgrimage in America. New York: Bantam Books, 1967.

Lindenmeyer, Otto. Black History: Lost, Stolen, or Strayed. New York: Avon Books, 1970.

Ludz, Peter C. "Alienation as a Concept in the Social Sciences." Current Sociology, 21 (1973), 15.

--- The German Democratic Republic from the Sixties to the Seventies: A Socio-Political Analysis. Cambridge, Mass.: Center for International Affairs, Harvard University, 1970.

--- Studien und Materialen zur Soziologie der DDR. Cologne and Opladen: Westdeutscher Verlag, 1964.

Lukacs, Georg. History and Class Consciousness: Studies in Marxist Dialectics. Cambridge: M.I.T. Press, 1971.

--- Realism in Our Time: Literature and the Class Struggle. New York: Harper and Row, 1972.

Marlow, H. Charleton, and Harrison M. Davis. The American Search for Woman. Santa Barbara: Clio Books, 1976.

Marx, Karl. "Theses On Feuerbach." In Marx and Engels: Basic Writings on Politics and Philosophy. Ed. Lewis Feuer. Garden City: Anchor Books/Doubleday, 1959.

Miller, Jeanne-Marie A. "Images of Black Women in Plays by Black Playwrights." College Language Association Journal, 22 (1977), 507.

Millett, Kate. Sexual Politics. New York: Ballantine Books, 1970.

Mohr, Heinrich. "Gerechtes Erinnern: Untersuchen zu Thema und Struktur von Hermann Kants Roman 'Die Aula' und einige Anmerkungen zu bundesrepublikanischen Rezensionen." Germanisch-romanische Monatsschrift, 22 (1974) 228.

Morrison, Toni. The Bluest Eye. New York: Holt, Rinehart, and Winston, 1970.

--- Song of Solomon. New York: Alfred A. Knopf, 1977.

--- Sula. New York: Alfred A. Knopf, 1973.

Muse, Benjamin. The American Negro Revolution: From Non-Violence to Black Power. New York: Citadel

Parrinder, Geoffrey. African Traditional Religion. New York: Harper and Row, 1962.

Plavius, Heinz. Kriterien und Kritik. Berlin: Hinstorff Verlag, 1977.

Powdermaker, Hortense. After Freedom. New York: Viking Press, 1939.

Pucket, Newbell N. Folk Beliefs of the Southern Negro. New York: Dover Publications, 1969.

Reinhardt, Kurt F. Germany: 2000 Years. New York: Frederick Unger, 1961.

Sander, Hans-Dietrich. Geschichte der schoenen Literatur in der DDR. Freiburg: Rombach, 1972.

Schubbe, Elimar, ed. Dokumente zur Kunst-Literatur- und Kulturpolitik in der SED, 1965-1971. Stuttgart: n.p., 1972.

Schwarz, David C. Political Alienation and Political Behavior. Chicago: Aldine Publishing Company, 1973.

Segall, Marshall H. Human Behavior and Public Policy. New York: Pergamon Press, 1976.

Sennett, Richard, and Jonathan Cobb. The Hidden Injuries of Class. New York: Vintage Books, 1973.

Smith, Jean E. Germany Beyond the Wall: People, Politics, and Prosperity. Boston: Little, Brown, 1967.

Smulkstys, Julius. Karl Marx. Boston: Twayne Publishers, 1974.

Sontheimer, Kurt, and Wilhelm Bleek. The Government and Politics of East Germany. London: Hutchinson University Library, 1975.

Spiewok, Wolfgang. "Hermann Kant." In Literatur der DDR. Ed. Hans-Juergen Geerdts. Stuttgart: Alfred Kroener, 1972.

Swingewood, Alan. The Novel and Revolution. New York: Barnes and Noble Books, 1975.

Tertz, Abram. On Socialist Realism. New York: Pantheon Books, 1960.

Thomas, Alexander, and Samuel Sillen. Racism and Psychiatry. New York: Brunner/Mozel, 1972.

Trager, Helen G., and Marian R. Yarrow. They Learn What They Live. New York: Harper, 1952.

Vivian, C. T. Black Power and the American Myth. Philadelphia: Fortress Press, 1970.

Walker, Alice. Meridian. New York: Pocket Books, 1972.

--- "My Father's Country Is the Poor." Black Scholar, Summer 1977, pp. 41-48.

--- The Third Life of Grange Copeland. New York: Harcourt, Brace, Jovanovich, 1970.

--- "The Unglamorous But Worthwhile Duties of the Black Revolutionary Artist or ... of the Black Writer Who Simply Works and Writes." Black Collegian, Sept.-Oct. 1971, pp. 43-47.

Washington, Mary H. "Black Women Image Makers." Black World, Aug. 1974, n. pag.

Weimann, Robert. Structure and Society in Literary History. Charlottesville: University of Virginia Press, 1976.

Wolf, Christa. The Reader and the Writer: Essays, Sketches, Memories. New York: International Publishers, 1977.

Woodward, Robert, and James J. Clark. The Social Rebel in American Literature. New York: Odyssey Press, 1968.

Young, Richard,P. Roots of Rebellion: The Evolution of Black Politics and Protest Since World War II. New York: Harper and Row, 1970.

Zaretsky, Eli. Capitalism, the Family and Personal Life. New York: Harper Colophon Books, 1976.